HOW TO
HAIKU

BRUCE ROSS

a writer's guide

to haiku

and related forms

TUTTLE PUBLISHING
Boston · Rutland, Vermont · Tokyo

First published in 2002 by Tuttle Publishing, an imprint of Periplus Editions (HK) Ltd., with editorial offices at 153 Milk Street, Boston, Massachusetts 02109.

Library of Congress Cataloging-in-Publication Data

Ross, Bruce, 1945–
    How to haiku : learning to write haiku, senryu, haibun, tanka, haiga, and renga / Bruce Ross.— 1st ed.
        p. cm.
    Includes bibliographical references.
    ISBN 0-8048-3232-3 (pbk.)
1. Haiku—Authorship. 2. Waka—Authorship. 3. Haibun—Authorship. I. Title.

PN1525 .R67 2001
808.1—dc21
                    00-060783

Distributed by

USA
Tuttle Publishing
Distribution Center
Airport Industrial Park
364 Innovation Drive
North Clarendon, VT 05759-9436
Tel: (802) 773-8930
Tel: (800) 526-2778

Japan
Tuttle Publishing
RK Building, 2nd Floor
2-13-10 Shimo-Meguro
Meguro-Ku, Tokyo 153 0064
Tel: 81-35-437-0171
Fax: 81-35-437-0755

Southeast Asia
Berkeley Books Pte. Ltd.
130 Soo Seng Road
#06-01/03 Olivine Building
Singapore 368357
Tel: (65) 280-1330
Fax: (65) 280-6290

First edition
06 05 04 03 02   10 9 8 7 6 5 4 3 2

Design by Gopa & Ted2

Printed in the United States of America

Acknowledgments

I would like to thank my students at Writers & Books, Rochester, New York; Writers at Champlain Mill, Winooski, Vermont; the Institute on Japan of the University of Vermont; the Doll-Anstadt Gallery, Burlington, Vermont; and the Japan-America Society of Vermont. Also, the comembers of the Haiku Poets of Upstate New York and the Burlington Haiku Group. And, finally, those haiku poets met in activities sponsored by Haiku Canada, the Haiku Society of America, the Boston Haiku Society, the Kaji Aso Studio, Boston, Massachusetts, and Haiku North America. Thanks for assistance are due to Francine Porad, John Stevenson, and Tomiko Hayashi. Thanks also are due to my editor, Jan Johnson, for nudging me in the right direction. Lastly, and most importantly, Astrid Calypso Miriam Andreescu, my wife; Murray David Ross, my brother; and Tom Clausen, my friend, well deserve very special thanks.

To my friends in the world haiku community.

A thousand bows to you.

Contents

Introduction

ONE EVENING I WAS WATCHING a program about elderly people who had problems with their bones. As part of their treatment they joined a class that practiced a form of T'ai Chi, the oriental exercise that has very slow and simple movements and looks like slow-motion dance. The version for these patients was even simpler. They stood straight up and moved their arms in a few easy patterns. In a later interview, one of the patients told how she broke into a sweat while doing the slow movements as if she had been playing tennis like she used to. She then commented: "It's very difficult to do something small in a meaningful way."

Haiku is like that. It is perhaps the smallest poetry form in the world, with about eight to twelve words in three short lines. Yet this tiny poem can say important things about how we feel about what we see around us. Haiku was invented hundreds of years ago in Japan. It was used to express feelings about nature, animals, and the seasons at a particular time and place and to share those feelings with others. So to write a haiku means to write about how you feel at a certain moment in time even if you are writing it down sometime after.

In the spring of 1999 the Burlington Haiku Group set up a haiku table at the Japan-America Society of Vermont's Japanese festival. A teenaged boy shrugged his shoulders when I asked him if he wanted to try writing a haiku. But he sat down and drew an empty couch to go with this haiku:

> nothing happening
> just another day
> nothing happening

I am sure we have all had one of these days. But we may not have been able to express this feeling as simply as this boy did. During that same spring, the children's librarian of Fletcher Free Library in Burlington, Vermont, held a haiku writing workshop for kids. Except for me and some mothers (to act as their children's scribes), all those who came to the workshop were kids seven to twelve years old. One young girl wrote this haiku:

> Birds in my backyard
> they sing sing sing all day long
> birds in my backyard

Another common experience: a bright spring day when the birds keep up their cheerful singing all day long, colorful spring flowers all around us. We know what the writer of this haiku felt.

Traditional Japanese haiku has two important parts. One is the joining of two images where you are really comparing the relationship between the two. This comparison is not like those we find in most poetry. We wouldn't say, "He looks like a monkey" in a haiku. Instead, we try to show what our feelings are by putting something we experienced together with another thing we experienced. We have a bad day so nothing is happening. Or nothing is happening because we are having a bad day. Tomorrow will probably be a better day. But today is a bad day. The other important part of traditional Japanese haiku is to connect our feelings to nature and the natural seasons. If we find a snowman, a Halloween costume, spring flowers, or a sandcastle in a haiku, we know what season that haiku is expressing. We know how that season feels. So if we find a snowman in a haiku we remember how winter feels. If birds are singing all day in a haiku, we know that it is spring, and we remember how spring feels.

Traditional Japanese haiku and all other haiku can express all kinds of feelings. Here is a haiku by the Japanese poet who is said to have created the haiku poem form:

stillness:
sinking into the rocks
a cricket's voice

—Bashō

We know from Bashō's journal that he was traveling around Japan when he wrote this. In summer he stopped to visit an ancient temple on a high mountain. This temple was noted for its peacefulness. Bashō wrote that there was absolute silence when he visited and that he was deeply moved by the experience. His haiku presents us with his feeling. He first names the silence that is the most important thing in this experience. The one sound, the cricket's chirp, makes the silence even greater. This small voice is powerful because it is the only sound. But this small voice is absorbed by the stillness of the rocks of the mountain and by the silence of the temple. Compare the kind of feeling in Bashō's haiku to one by an American haiku poet:

Christmas Eve . . .
at the lot, the trees
not chosen

—Tom Tico

We all know the happiness of being with our families on Christmas Eve. Almost everyone is at home relaxing with a festive meal and the promise of gifts. We are also supposed to feel goodwill toward everyone. But for one reason or another some people are left out of this celebration. The leftover Christmas trees remind us of those people. This haiku leaves us with a deep feeling of sadness by connecting this holiday night of expectation, celebration, and reverence to an image of something left out.

Haiku can also offer a playful feeling. Here is another cricket poem. The author is also one of the great early Japanese haiku masters:

I am going out . . .
be good and play together,
my cricket children

—Issa

We know from Issa's biography, and especially from his haiku, that although he led a hard life he had a childlike disposition. He loved farm animals, pets, flowers, and even insects. He felt so close to these things that he treated them as he treated his own family and friends. In many of his haiku he talks to animals. He may not be talking to them the way we talk to each other, but his concern for them is, in a way, like talking. Issa lived in a simple village home that sometimes had one or another kind of insect also living there. These insects became part of his family because he cared about them. So in this haiku Issa talks to them like he would talk to his own children. And we feel the playfulness of his love for these creatures. Compare the kind of feeling in Issa's haiku to one by another American haiku poet:

waving back
at the poppy field
the retarded child

—vincent tripi

This author is not trying to make fun of this child. He is, like Issa, celebrating the love of a human being for a nonhuman living thing. Poppies have big, bright red or orange blossoms. They are cheerful-looking. And when the wind blows through them they might even appear to a child as innocent as this one as if they are waving. Just as many of us have smiled when we've seen very small children talk to their pets and stuffed animals, we can smile at the celebration of innocence in the playful exchange between this child and the field of flowers.

Haiku is not like most poetry. It is not trying to present strong emotion through made-up comparisons and imaginative expression. Rather, it is trying to present feelings through images that wer part of an experience. The Japanese use the word *aware* when they discuss how poetry works. It means "sadness" but is often used to mean "to be touched" by something. Haiku is based on this phrase. We are touched by something and it causes us to have feelings. We then share those feelings through haiku. If we are successful, the reader will experience the feeling we had when we composed the haiku. Yet an important part of a successful haiku is how we have our feelings. In a way, in haiku, the mind directs the heart, if we think of our minds as giving special attention to things and our hearts as pure feeling. So when we make a haiku, we are not merely using physical images taken from our experiences to express our feeling. Instead, we are letting our attention lead us to our feeling, and the images we choose for our haiku express that feeling. So writing haiku is not some kind of excitement but a concentration on everyday life. The German poet Rainer Maria Rilke wrote letters of advice to a young man who was trying to write poetry. Rilke said that the young poet should try "being close to things" even if he was feeling a bit suppressed by the world. He added that children were still the same as when he was a child, sad and happy. He also wrote that you "go up" in your encounter with things. In writing haiku, we might say that we do not use our minds as we usually do. Instead, we are trying to be as open to the "things" of the world as little children are, and to have the same kind of simple happy and sad feelings little children have. When we do this we are not using the intellectual part of the mind that reasons things out. Nor are we using the part that is our imagination to make things up. If we can do this, we are able to experience pure feeling in the world around us. And this feeling will lead to a sense of love and compassion for the things of our world, including each other, like Issa's love for the crickets or vincent tripi's love of the child waving to the poppies. If we tone down our own personality, what is called our ego, we can develop the kind of attention that haiku needs. The world of things will open up to us, and our feelings for those things will lead us to compassion. So, in a sense, we are not racing after feeling with our mind and our imagination but letting go so that feeling can come to us. If this happens we "go up" with feeling. And this feeling, like all feeling in haiku, is in the present moment. It is not our strong emotion. It is not our creative imagination. It is a heartfelt presentation of feelings for what is happening here and now at this present time. It is "just another day," birds singing in a backyard, stillness, unsold trees on Christmas Eve, house crickets, and a child waving to flowers.

It is obvious from the examples of haiku by Tom Tico and vincent tripi, as well as that by the teenaged boy and the young schoolgirl, that American English can movingly express feeling through this tiny Japanese poem form. And today, American haiku is in fact practiced in each of the fifty states and by people of all ages. Here are two haiku, one by a two-and-a-half-year-old and the other by a ninety-four-year-old, that were both published in a haiku journal:

outside—	convalescence
the rain flutters	this spring
on the pavement	unexpected
—Emma Clausen	—Oliver K. Blackburn

I may have even published a haiku by the youngest person ever. I was leading a haiku writing party for the Japan-America Society of Vermont. We were celebrating the full autumn moon during September 1999 and writing about it. One of our members had brought his ten-month-old daughter and "translated" her haiku for me. I published it along with others in my "Haiku Corner" column of the Japan-America Society of Vermont Newsletter:

> me, La La & Mommie
> watching the moon
> with all my friends
>
> —Emi Borch

I may have also published one of the earliest haiku written in America. At the same festival where I met the author of "just another day," I met a woman who told me her grandmother wrote haiku in the early part of the twentieth century. She remembered this wonderful haiku by her grandmother, which I published in "Haiku Corner":

> hayloft long empty
> horses, cows, and bawling calves
> leave haunting fragrance
>
> —Alice Robinson Durgin

There are four stages in the development of American haiku. Each stage may be said to explore the nature of the poetic image. The first stage began during the 1910s and 1920s, the time Alice Robinson Durgin wrote her haiku, and continued into the 1930s and 1940s. It centered on a group of poets who associated themselves with a movement called Imagism. One of its leaders, Ezra Pound, defined poetry as "an intellectual and emotional complex in an instant of time." Others in this group, like Amy Lowell, Hilda Doolittle, and John Gould Fletcher, were, like Pound, influenced by Japanese poetry. They wanted to express their feelings in concrete natural images. William Carlos Williams extended this interest to concentrate on the inner life of things, like the objects in his well-known poem "The Red Wheel Barrow." Wallace Stevens, on the other hand, concentrated on the mental attention of the poet, as he does in his portrait of winter emptiness, "The Snow Man," and in his haikulike "Thirteen Ways of Looking at a Blackbird." The second stage of American haiku took place in the fifties and centered on the poets Gary Snyder, Allen Ginsberg, and Jack Kerouac, who were part of what was called the Beat Movement. They were more interested in ordinary experience than in imaginatively constructed poetry and wrote haiku about kicking an icebox door shut or turning around to see cherry petals falling on their back. The third stage centers on *The Haiku Anthology* (1974), a collection of American and Canadian haiku poets, many of whom were influenced by Japanese haiku and writing about Japanese haiku. Many of these poets, like Nick Virgilio, James William Hackett, Cor van den Heuvel, and Anita Virgil, were able to compose haiku deep in present tense feeling. The fourth stage of American haiku, which extends from the late 1970s to the present, has explored many kinds of experimental haiku forms and approaches. Yet it has also produced wonderful nature haiku by Charles Dickson and John Wills and insights into human nature by Alexis Rotella. And more and more the language of this stage is fresh-sounding and almost musical.

A contemporary American haiku poet can feel that he or she is part of a community. There are haiku clubs in many parts of the United States, haiku newsletters and journals, national contests and organizations, and even electronic chat rooms. And if an American haiku poet desires, he or she can even be part of a worldwide haiku community. Haiku is now being written on every continent except Antarctica. In southeastern Europe, haiku appears to be the most widely written form of poetry. In fact, it is possible, given that most American students have been asked to write at least one haiku, and that millions of Japanese write haiku, that haiku may be the most widely written specific form of poetry in the world. A number of wonderful haiku journals are presently being published in many languages, usually with English translations. And there are frequent international haiku meetings and contests.

What does the birth country of haiku—Japan—think of all this? Well, they are even busier with haiku activity than the international haiku community. There are thousands of haiku groups and up to five million haiku poets in Japan. Office workers take an hour or two off to go for a haiku walk. Leading newspapers have daily haiku columns. You can find haiku on a box of tea or on the side of a bus. I think the Japanese are amused at the worldwide interest in haiku. But there are already Japanese journals and newspapers publishing American and international haiku, and meetings between Japanese haiku poets and American and international haiku poets. There are also Japanese web sites in English. Yet a common theme of Japanese writing about international haiku is that it should develop within the context of a country's own language and culture. After all, a haiku is what is happening in a certain place at a certain time. Although there are universal aspects to nature and humanity, the subjects of haiku, haiku is poetry of the particular. Therefore the Japanese believe a student's task is to explore the particulars in his or her daily life and to express those feelings in his or her own language. But concentration on these particulars, these moments that are haiku, could be even more important. As a modern Zen master living in America has said, "When you understand one thing through and through, you understand everything." By focusing on the things around them, one at a time, in the language they know, students can learn deep and wonderful, and sometimes playful, things about nature and human life.

Looking at Nature: Haiku

WHEN WE WRITE A HAIKU, we are performing a balancing act. On the one hand we are trying to present the deep feeling we experienced, on the other hand we are describing what we saw. What we felt and what we saw are not necessarily the same thing. To put it another way: what we experience is a result of how we feel or think about things, but how we express what we experience comes from physical images.

For example, I was taking a hike with my brother one spring day in a nature preserve on Cape Cod. We were enjoying the sights, sounds, and smells of the new season. We came to a small pond. Near its middle was a log. I sensed something at one end of it. Turtles! When I looked more closely I noticed two of them leaning against each other. All this happened in a moment. I composed the following haiku:

> Head against head
> two spring turtles sunning
> on a log

What was I feeling? I was feeling that all of nature was alive on this bright morning in the woods. I was feeling the incredible presence of some turtles sitting so still on a log. And most wonderfully I was delighted when I saw that the two turtles were leaning their heads against each other. They seemed almost human as they sat there like this. My haiku should convey some of this feeling—such is the purpose of haiku. But to do this I had to use concrete images: the turtles, their touching heads, and the glorious spring day. And while I wanted to present a picture of the scene, I didn't want to present one that was too realistic. I merely wanted to use images that would depict the important elements and suggest what I felt. The words used and their phrasing helped to do this. That is, there is sound and there is rhythm in this haiku.

HISTORY AND FORM OF HAIKU

The man who coined the word *haiku* and who started modern haiku writing in Japan in the early twentieth century was named Shiki. He said that haiku should be a "sketch from nature." But what could this mean? His two most well known students provide us with an explanation. One of them, Kyoshi, thought haiku should reflect a person's feelings for nature, and his own haiku are filled with sensitive responses to nature. The other student, Hekigodō, thought haiku should be realistic, and he urged his students to pay attention to details. Hekigodō also thought that anything could be a subject of haiku, whether it be one's own moody thoughts or something that was not particularly beautiful. And he believed that nature does not have to be an important part of a haiku. So at the beginning of modern haiku we find two opposite ways of expressing ourselves: feeling what we experience, particularly in nature, and realistically describing what we experience, whatever that might be. Both types of haiku continue to be written, but those who base their haiku on feelings in nature identify with Kyoshi, the founder of traditional haiku.

ELEMENTS OF TRADITIONAL HAIKU

The essence of traditional haiku consists of two things. First, there is an association with nature through one of the seasons either by naming the season (*kigo*), like winter or spring, or by suggesting the season through specific elements of that season (*kidai*), like a frozen pond or cherry blossoms. There are even books in Japan (*saijiki*) that list these elements by season so that haiku poets can look up a seasonal topic for inspiration or check to see that they have got their subjects in the right season. The second essential part of traditional haiku is setting up a relationship between two images and separating those images with a punctuation mark (*kireji*). In Japanese, these marks are really words that show emotion, like "ah." Because most traditional Japanese poetry was written in phrases of five or seven syllables, and haiku came from a stanza of poetry of three lines of phrases in a five, seven, five order, most haiku in English is written in three lines. The first line in traditional Japanese haiku usually carries a seasonal reference and ends with the punctuation mark. So line one presents one image and lines two and three combine to make another image. The kireji is thus an emotional and linguistic break that creates an "internal comparison." This "internal comparison" supplies the dynamic feeling for many haiku. American haiku therefore is also written in three lines with a break after the first line.

HAIKU AS NATURE POETRY

Most American haiku is also connected with nature even though many American haiku writers live in cities. After all, snow falls on a city, and even Southern states have spring flowers. Traditional Japanese poetry is said to be about "birds and flowers." And in fact most of the world's poetry from time immemorial has been about nature. In the nineteenth century, a group of American writers developed a philosophy of life and art that was based on nature. Their leader, Ralph Waldo Emerson, felt that there was a "fundamental unity" between humanity and nature, that we gain something important through nature. If fact, Emerson's secretary, Henry David Thoreau, lived for two years in a small cabin in the woods to try to learn all he could from nature. His record of those two years, his well-known *Walden*, reveals the wonder and spiritual truth he found there. Thoreau called for a change in human feeling to one that was more a childlike openness to experience, and he based this change on an Emersonian exchange with nature, not upon the workaday world of the city. Accordingly, a contemporary

American haiku poet has even suggested that haiku, through nature, can heal the problems of society. If we remember that the Japanese word used for haiku feeling, *aware*, means "to be touched by" something in nature, we can see that the receptiveness Thoreau called for is similar to traditional haiku's regard for nature. Here are some examples of haiku that perfectly reflect such receptiveness to nature:

touch of dawn
the snail withdraws
its horns

—John Wills

through falling snow,
the pale form of a snow goose—
trumpeting

—Carol Field

wolf spider dancing
sideways on the wall

dusk

—Michael McNierney

Opening its eyes
closing its eyes
a cat in the sun

—Arizona Zipper

dusk   from rock to rock a waterthrush

—John Wills

Yet how can haiku about the same old snow or the same old spring flowers be good poetry? Ezra Pound, one of the leaders of the Imagist poets, said of poetry that you should "make it new." You need to express experience in a fresh way to make it moving. No more same old same old. No more "roses are red, violets are blue." Kyoshi put it this way: "Deep is new." But what does it mean to be deep? Two of my favorite haiku show us what kind of feeling haiku should have. One is a moody poem about autumn, and the other is a tender poem about a pet dog:

Autumn twilight:
  the wreath on the door
    lifts in the wind

    —Nick Virgilio

middle of the highway
with bells on
our old dog

    —Carol Montgomery

The first looks like a traditional haiku. It has a season name, "autumn," a line break with a punctuation mark, and two images, "twilight" and the wreath in the wind. There is an undeniable feeling of sadness in this poem. It takes place during the season when most plants and the leaves on the trees wither and die, and many animals migrate or hibernate. People are beginning to prepare for winter, too. It is also the time between day and night, which emphasizes the dramatic changes brought on by autumn. The wreath seems to have a life of its own. But like the leaves that are stirred in the autumn wind, it stirs, too. We know somehow that these leaves will fall and dry up on the ground. A sense of our mortality and our frailty seems to pervade the haiku. This haiku is a good example of one kind of feeling the Japanese value in haiku. They call it *sabi*, which is a kind of moody loneliness that can be found in experience. It is not something we would call depressing; rather, it is an expression of some deep truth about things. Notice, also, the serious tone achieved through the choice of stark words and actions. The second haiku looks and sounds like a modern poem. There is no real season connection; here, the connection with nature is directly presented by the dog. There is no line break after the first line because there is really only one image: an old dog in the middle of the street. And this image is really one sentence pared down a little. This image becomes a poem through the way the three phrases of the three lines are set up and expressed. The phrases sound conversational. "With bells on" sometimes means to arrive at a celebration in a good mood, dressed up, and on time. You don't sense the dog is in any danger, particularly because of this phrase, which adds a bit of humor to the haiku. This haiku conveys the deep sense of love and compassion that the author has for her dog. It also is a good example of another Japanese haiku value, *karumi* or "lightness," a warm, homey treatment of familiar things, like this old dog. This value is also related to the Japanese idea of *wabi*, the quiet beauty of ordinary things, like an old flower pot.

Here are some examples of sabi-, karumi-, and wabi-filled haiku. First are haiku that capture moments of deep loneliness in which a profound stillness seems to surround things:

a stick goes over the falls at sunset

—Cor van den Heuvel

melting snow
the sun shines into the back
of an empty truck

—Cor van den Heuvel

first flakes
a sparrow settles deeper
into its feathers

—Frank K. Robinson

twilight deepens
the wordless things
I know

—Francine Porad

Sunset . . .
the scarecrow stretches
across the field

—Leroy Kanterman

There, by the roadside
a family of crosses
in the fading light

—Joan C. Sauer

Unlike the lonely sadness of sabi that surrounds itself in unmoving timelessness, which the simple actions in a haiku only intensify, karumi and wabi hint at the wonderful liveliness beneath the surface of ordinary things:

only a shanty
but these roses here
beside the door . . .

—Hal Roth

The whole neighborhood—
Plum blossoms,
Burnt toast . . .

—Miriam Sagan

the neglected garden growing faster than ever

—Molly Magner

cloudy day half a load of clothes in the wash

—Marlene Mountain

in the house plants
daddy longlegs
has found a winter home

—Raffael de Gruttola

old white dogwood
white again
with new snow

—Thom Williams

Though feeling in haiku can be deep, even lively, it can also provide humor. I offer two of my own, one from autumn and one from spring, as examples:

country farm market
a scarecrow waving from
the pumpkin field

bright spring day
a table of beanie babies
on a front lawn

One day as I was driving down a country road, I noticed a very small farm market by the side of the road. Vegetables, including a huge pile of pumpkins, were displayed in boxes in front of the market. I realized that the pumpkin field from which the pumpkins came was right beside the market. I glanced back to the field and saw the scarecrow waving at me. I have often driven by a house that, on nice days, had a table of something for sale. One day I looked closely. In sitting positions on little shelves were all kinds of Beanie Babies. It was early spring and I thought these Beanie Babies almost sprouted up like colorful new spring flowers. There is an element here of what is called a "found poem," when we respond to a humanly constructed experience or thing, like the scarecrow or the table of Beanie Babies. And such "found poetry," whatever it happens to be, can also inspire a serious treatment, like the following, which I wrote one winter when, after hiking down a long sweltering trail in a tropical forest on St. John Island, I came to the ocean:

> NO CRAB HUNTING:
> all the silent holes beneath
> the shining rocks

HAIKU WRITING GUIDELINES

There are a number of important points to consider when you write haiku. The first point is: *Haiku takes place in the present.* This is its special feature. Unlike most poetry, which exists in the mind of its author, haiku embodies a feeling experienced in a moment of time. You write the haiku because you want to share that feeling with others. But since your haiku exists in the present, you need to be careful of your phrasing. For example, you should avoid adding "-ing" to your verbs. If you don't, you will be placing an artificial emphasis on your very small poem. But while your haiku exists in the present, you may want to include a reference to the past if it somehow connects with your haiku's present and doesn't overpower it.

A haiku, however, is not merely a description of something that is happening in the present. This is the second point: *A haiku is a moment of awareness, insight, surprise, or delight.* This is what adds depth of feeling to haiku. For example, you might find delight in the inner life of a caterpillar's existence or gain philosophic insight into the meaning of death by watching the falling autumn leaves. In order to do this you must *deemphasize your ego.* Your subject—not your usual old self—is what focuses a haiku. Therefore, try not to overuse the pronoun "I." And although you should not use the strong emotions we associate with the everyday self, you should include human nature as it relates to your haiku. The idea is to open your mind to experience and not let it be filled with your emotions. This is what makes haiku different from other poetry. You are not using your imagination to stir up emotion as you do in other poetry. Therefore you should *deemphasize figurative "poetic" expressions* such as metaphors, similes, and personifications. You should also avoid dramatic sound values like rhyme, assonance, and dissonance. Like other elements, "poetic" expression would overpower the small haiku poem. So haiku is not really a tiny lyric poem.

Haiku is most usually connected with nature. A season word or a concrete representation connects us to a world of which we are a part but is greater than us. This connection adds depth to our experience. It also, as in most poetry, offers us an experience of beauty and, beyond that, insight. Although the Japanese identify the natural world through their particular seasons (kigo) and season words (kidai), if we take the time, wherever we live, we can identify our own seasons and season words.

When we actually write down our haiku they are in three lines of about twelve to fourteen syllables in a *short-long-short pattern*. The three phrases of five, seven, and five syllables in Japanese haiku, which were often written in a straight line, became the short-long-short lines of American haiku, although American haiku sometimes takes other forms, including a one-line haiku. Most of these three-line American haiku line up on their left margin, although there is much variation in the patterning of a haiku's lines, sometimes to reinforce the meaning of a haiku through a visual effect. In addition, most American haiku go without capitalization of any words, except proper names, although some American haiku poets begin their haiku with a capital letter and end it with a period, and some capitalize the first letter in each of the three lines. Also, most American haiku does away with end punctuation, although many use some kind of punctuation between two images in their haiku.

A haiku usually contains one or two images. If there were more, a haiku would be cluttered. The two images of a haiku are usually separated by an explicit break with a punctuation mark like a dash (—), a period (.), an ellipsis (. . .), a colon (:), a semicolon (;), an exclamation point (!), a comma (,), or a question mark (?). But sometimes they are separated by an implicit break without any punctuation mark. In Japanese haiku the break is called a kireji and is actually like a combination of an emotional word and a punctuation mark like *kana* ("Ah!" or "Oh!"). The image, both the idea it is representing and the way it is phrased in words, is important because it conveys what your haiku experience was and how you felt about that experience. So you will want to create precise and pure images that get to the point and reflect your feeling without excess words and in just the right phrasing. And if there are two images or more, there needs to be a perfect balance and interrelationship among them. You cannot simply throw two interesting images together, even if you experienced them together. There needs to be some kind of inner necessity for the images to be joined.

Your haiku should have varying tone. You may be serious or you may be playful. You may have a formal voice to add appropriate depth to a profound subject. Or you may have a speaking voice that phrases your images in a conversational manner to bring your reader closer to some everyday experience that you have seen in a new light.

Remember that haiku is not merely description. You are not taking a snapshot of an object or a scene. Rather, you are expressing the feeling that you had while experiencing that object or scene. Your choice of words, phrasing, and tone make a haiku far more than a description. Also, *your haiku is not a little drama.* You are not orchestrating something by putting this image with that image for dramatic effect like a stage director. There should be a naturalness to what happens in a haiku. You are not trying for a cause-and-effect relationship between your images. Nor should you impose artificial tension in your haiku. Your experience happened without any manipulation on your part, and this should show in your haiku.

Your feeling in haiku should be pure and sincere. Therefore you should *avoid sentimentality.* The haiku should not reflect what we think we should be feeling or what others have told us we should be feeling. We want to stay away from affected or exaggerated emotion. And we should avoid clichéd expression and feeling that is trite or overused. Remember, each haiku represents a new experience. Even if you have seen the snow fall or the spring flowers bloom year after year, you can still be moved by them. You must not fall into the trap of saying that there is nothing new under the sun. Rather, remember Ezra Pound's wise statement concerning poetry: "Make it new!" and Kyoshi's advice for haiku: "Deep is new."

Finally, *do not explain anything*. To paraphrase a familiar advertising slogan, let your images do the talking. In haiku you do not explain how your experience felt. How you express your images will do this for you.

It might be helpful to compare my guidelines with a discussion of haiku composition that accompanied an entrance form to an international Japanese haiku contest:

> Haiku are short, imagistic poems about the things that make people feel connected to nature. In Japanese, haiku traditionally have seventeen short sounds divided into three lines of a 5–7–5 syllable pattern with the middle line longer than the first and third lines. . . . Most though not all haiku reflect nature or one of the four seasons. The words of haiku should evoke in the reader the emotion felt by the poet, and should not describe merely the emotion. Effective power of poetic device in language comes from simplicity, elegance and concentration in mind. You are suggested not to repeat words or ideas which convey the same meaning or feeling. That is, you should avoid redundancy.

As you see, I have covered most of the haiku composition issues presented here. Although I had discussed the idea of feeling in response to a connection with nature (*aware*) and the special focus and concentration of the mind as a kind of openness to nature earlier, I would add these to my guidelines. I would also add the idea of elegance, what I call polish, in haiku. There should be a perfect balance in the images, ideas, phrasing, word choice, and sound. Nothing could be added and nothing could be taken away from such a haiku. A simple test for elegance is to try to rearrange the order of your lines. Your original order should be the only way to perfectly reflect your feeling. You might try this test with any word that may seem possibly unnecessary to your haiku. If your haiku sounds more polished to you without that word, then you should leave it out.

The next issue is about repetition. Obviously, in such a small poem, repetition would unbalance the haiku. So if you mention snow in a haiku, you probably don't need to use the word *winter* also. However, in some cases you might want to distinguish, say, spring snow from winter snow. Also, you might want to use some similar idea, key word, or image to create a special emphasis or focus in your haiku.

These guidelines are helpful because it isn't easy to write a perfect haiku. Bashō, perhaps Japan's greatest haiku writer, said that if someone writes one or two such haiku over a lifetime, that person is a haiku master. This is not to scare anyone away from writing haiku. Haiku are fun and they can teach us important things about ourselves and the world around us. But in working with many students writing haiku and in observing my own development in haiku writing, I have noticed some common patterns in which earlier haiku are not as strong as later haiku. This is not to say that someone cannot start writing great haiku right off the bat. I have seen this. But most haiku writers, even the great masters, have had to develop their craft.

SILENCE

One of the most common characteristics of haiku, as you can see from the many examples I have so far presented, is silence. Both sabi and wabi are associated with silence and stillness, and sabi is sometimes defined as quietness. Why is silence so important to haiku? At the most obvious level it allows us to focus our mind and therefore be more attentive and receptive to our experience and feeling. If you walk into a park or a woods and then just still yourself and still your thoughts, you will be surprised at what you will begin to observe and respond to. The same thing will happen if you walk into a garden or onto a sidewalk or into a room in your house. Still, as you can see from many of the examples, haiku silence is often connected with nature. This is because nature has a way of taking us out of our usual self. It helps slow down our busy thoughts and allows us to pay attention to the little things in nature, like dew on a caterpillar's back, and the great things in nature, like the stillness of a snow-covered field in the moonlight. And further, silence in nature can lead to spiritual revelation. This is why Bashō visited the mountaintop temple where he heard the cricket, and saw other scenes in nature on his long walking trip around Japan. This is why Thoreau lived in a small cabin in the woods for two years. What they experienced was filled with such revelation that their journals became classics of world literature: *Narrow Path to the Interior* and *Walden*. Here are some modern American haiku examples of this kind of silence. Note how what little movement there is in these poems makes us more aware of the greater silence and stillness, like the temple cricket in Bashō's poem:

Autumn afternoon—
without a ripple three clouds
cross the pond

  —Patricia Neubauer

Dusk over the lake;
a turtle's head emerges
then silently sinks

  —Virgil Hutton

dusk—
fog fills a valley
filled with snow

  —Jeff Witkin

the bright silence of sun in a clay pot

  —Geraldine C. Little

You should also note that even when the words *silence* or *stillness* are used in a haiku, like Bashō's use of "stillness" in his haiku, it is the particular concrete image, like Bashō's cricket, that makes us respond to the deep intuitive feeling in a haiku.

HAIKU IMAGES

We all know the expression "pretty as a picture." The poems of the Imagists were often works in which their feelings were put into pictures. And while there is a kind of beauty in these pictures, it is not haiku. Haiku is not a pretty picture. The images of haiku support a deeper level of feeling than this, and are of utmost importance because they act as a go-between that connects the *phrasing* of the haiku's words to the *insight* of the haiku's words. The image is both a picture and an idea, and a good haiku will perfectly combine the two. In such a haiku the phrasing of the picture and the idea will have a polished rhythm and sound. All the elements that are centered on the image will evoke a feeling for the reader to experience. And in a good haiku that feeling offers insight. Look at how the images in the following haiku provide insight. In poetry, the most common figurative expression is metaphor. One thing is connected to another to provide an image of how the poem's author was feeling. In haiku, we have what might be called "absolute metaphor." The images in a haiku are not so much compared as linked. And in a good haiku there is an intuitive rightness about this link. We can't explain this link in a rational way, but we can certainly feel its rightness:

migrating geese—
once there was so much
to say

—Adele Kenny

a passing shower
white spider chrysanthemum
with tangled petals

—Brent Partridge

dawn
a broken line of shoes
on the temple steps

—paul m.

Each of these haiku offers a deep insight into the natural order of change in nature and humanity: migrating geese, chrysanthemum petals after rain, a crooked line of shoes at dawn. Even if Adele Kenny is commenting on the image of the geese, she isn't really telling us how she feels as much as showing her response to the geese. There is an implicit sense of realization of and surrender to the natural order of things here. The next two haiku also reveal how change and even seeming disorder are also a part of that natural order. The white chrysanthemum blossoms are beautiful with their long, bright, even petals before the rain, and they are just as beautiful when those petals are tangled up after the rain. The shoes in the last haiku are left on the temple steps while their owners are offering morning prayers or simply meditating. We sometimes think of spiritual experience as something orderly and perfect. But after all, we are only human. And that, too, is part of our spirituality, so wonderfully evoked in the line of uneven shoes.

OUR SENSES AND HAIKU

Part of being human is to experience the world around us with our senses. Even if we are told to monitor, figuratively, what we think, feel, or say—like the three wise monkeys who see no evil, hear no evil, and speak no evil—we know that our senses are important. Most poetry, including haiku, is based upon senses. They provide us with our images and insights. They also bring a concrete liveliness to haiku in a concentrated way, unlike most other poetry. It might be helpful to remember this when we compose haiku even though it should be obvious that haiku poets depend on the senses. Let us look at some examples. The expression "at first glance" tells us how important sight is to experience. We are also told that "seeing is believing." But in haiku, how we see is as important as what we see:

by their winter lights
across the way
I feel I know them

    —Thom Williams

The time it takes—
for snowflakes to whiten
the distant pines

    —Lorraine Ellis Harr

Notice the subtlety and ambiguity of the image of winter lights. One senses that the author is looking at these lights on a still winter night and that their brightness provides a kind of fellowship for the person looking at them. Notice another kind of subtlety that incorporates the passing of time in the sad moodiness of snow on the distant pines.

In haiku we don't abuse sound by speaking too much, like an unwise monkey. Rather, we are attentive to the kinds of sound that will reveal something to us about nature or our own natures:

out of the fog bank
    croak
of a snowy egret

    —Charles Dickson

autumn drizzle—
the slow ticking
of the clock

    —Bruce Ross

We are often surprised by nature. Though Charles Dickson may not be able to see the beautiful white egret through the fog, he can remember its beauty in this haunting example of nature's hiddenness. In the second haiku the dreariness of the autumn drizzle is only intensified by the sound of the clock, which seems subjectively to slow down time.

Taste and smell are two of our most primitive senses, yet they give us undeniable pleasure through food and drink and flowers and perfume. But in haiku we connect these senses to a more delicate feeling or some larger connection with nature:

morning tea—
dew on the edges
of the kitchen window

    —Jason Murray

marshmallows melt
in the steaming cocoa
midnight rain

    —Joyce Austin Gilbert

carved wooden bowl
the smell of pears
ripening

    —Karen Klein

so round moon—
the slow stirring
of mulled cider

    —Tony Pupello

Our cups of tea often have little bubbles on their edges. Notice how these bubbles and the tea's wetness connect with the dew on the window. The tea warms us, and if it is cold outside, the steam from the tea may condense on the window like dew. On a cold rainy night nothing cheers us up like the sweet rich taste of cocoa and marshmallows, which you can practically taste in the second haiku. The smell of ripening pears may be even sweeter. These pears get softer and softer and the hardness of the wooden bowl reminds us even more of this. Notice the polish of the image and its phrasing in this haiku. The smell of warm spiced cider is intoxicating and serves as a background to the linking of the roundness of the moon to the circular motions of stirring the cider, as if the stirrer were unconsciously trying to draw that perfectly round moon.

Touch is one of the most intimate of senses when it occurs between two people, but the feel of textures is pleasant in itself and may sometimes connect us to the life of things in nature:

crabapple petals everywhere
I brush one
from her cheek

    —Larry Kimmel

a cloud on the water
I float half-submerged
with the frogs

    —Larry Gates

The first haiku has a nice polish to its phrasing. Nothing could be added or subtracted. The feeling the author has for the other person has a quietly understated tone that comes through perfectly in the phrasing. We know how soft a flower petal is, and this softness is linked to the author's gentle movement and tender feeling. In the second haiku the author feels how clouds float in the air and frogs float in the water. There is a lighthearted tone to this haiku, a tone that evokes how a human being can effortlessly fit in with the things of nature.

A final sense is one not normally thought of as a sense. We are told to watch what we say and to clear our minds. In other words, we should try to be levelheaded and to control our emotions. But sometimes our thoughts and our emotions take us over. A goal in haiku is to have a precise mental focus when we experience and compose haiku. The deepness of a haiku's expressed feeling is usually a product of such mental focus. We have toned down our thoughts and our emotions. We have become receptive to the feelings in a given circumstance or experience. But sometimes a haiku can be about the inability to clear one's mind:

Among leafless trees   angry at them too
    too many thoughts   for challenging my mood
    in my head   crabapple blossoms

        —David Elliott   —Charles Trumbull

If Adele Kenny's migrating geese haiku is about resigning oneself to nature's rhythms—in other words, clearing one's mind of thoughts and emotions and our usual everyday self—then these haiku reflect the inability to see an important truth about nature even when it is in front of one's nose or, in these cases, above one's head. In the first haiku the author cannot understand that he should unburden himself of that with which he is obsessed. There is a subtle, and possibly witty, comparison of the empty trees and his full mind, of the fallen leaves and his numerous thoughts. In the next haiku, which is quite amusing, the author's emotion is so strong that it cannot be stopped even by the beautiful blossoms that he can't but notice.

THE HAIKU MOMENT

The ideal for the haiku poet's mind, however, in experiencing and composing what has been called the "haiku moment," is a controlled receptiveness to, particularly, nature. Consider this classic haiku by a modern American haiku poet:

> moonlight—
> a sand dune
> shifts
>
> —Virginia Brady Young

Here the subjective everyday self does not interfere with the particular profound silence that surrounds the beach. Despite the movement of the sand, we sense a profound stillness in this scene as well as emptiness. The observer is probably the only person around, yet we don't really sense her presence itself. This haiku has a rich sense of sabi loneliness that is a form of the most deep and subtle kind of beauty.

RESPONDING TO THE HAIKU OF OTHERS

Our haiku moments, like the exquisite one below, are meant to be shared with others. And sometimes a haiku will move us so much that we might want to respond to it with one of our own. Let us look again at this haiku by Cor van den Heuvel:

> a stick goes over the falls at sunset

Now compare it to this one:

nothing,
at the moment,
flowing over the falls

—John Stevenson

I do not know if this haiku was written in response to the first one, but the echoes of the first are undeniable. And it is in fact a kind of poetic response to the feeling of loneliness in the first, though with a less stark phrasing, which, in itself, is a kind of response.

There is a prize-winning haiku filled with sabi by Ebba Story that I have written about. I was very moved by this haiku's feeling. It probably echoed in my mind with an image in my poem "A Dirge for the Great Mother":

two stray salmon, lost puppies
looking for their mother,
slowly hunt for the channel
up the Genesee.

Here is the haiku:

peeping . . . peeping
the lost duckling's wake
through the shadows

—Ebba Story

Several years after I read this haiku I was camping on a lake in northern Vermont near the Canadian border. One evening I sat beside the lake at sunset almost meditating. As it got darker I noticed some small forms moving across the water. I looked more closely and experienced this:

mountain dusk . . .
a duck and her ducklings glide
into the shadows

I was not consciously thinking about Ebba Story's haiku when I composed this haiku, but sometime after I wrote it I realized that there might be a subconscious response to her poem in it—really an answer to the plight of her duckling.

In the winter of the year 2000 I was snowshoeing on the Appalachian Trail in southern Vermont. It was a bright day. The sky was blue and the line of clouds was sparkling white. It reminded me of a well-known haiku by one of the early great American haiku poets— it has even been put on a T-shirt:

the hills
release the summer clouds
one   by one   by one

—John Wills

When I reached an open ridge I turned around to look at the landscape. I was facing south, toward another mountain, when I experienced this:

blue sky
cloud after cloud from behind
the snowy mountain

As I composed the haiku in my head I knew I was responding to the cloud haiku by John Wills. I was not doing it in a directly conscious way, but I knew I was responding to, as well as echoing his poem. And if I were to publish my haiku I would want to include at its bottom "—for John Wills."

HAIKU SEQUENCES

Finally, you might find that a certain experience or location inspires you to compose more than one haiku about the same subject. As long as there is no obvious repetition of images, except for the one that unites the haiku, you might produce a successful haiku sequence where the haiku are linked to each other by a common theme and tone. In 1993 I attended a haiku conference at Los Pasitos College in California. I stood for a long time on the glazed-tile walk staring at the Los Pasitos hills and at the crows that were walking around in a gently sloping field of grass just in front of me. I can't remember now, but I probably composed the haiku in the following sequence as I experienced them:

BLACKBIRDS

still summer evening—
the blackbird's underfeather
floats down

Los Pasitos hills—
two blackbirds standing apart
on the grass

afternoon sunlight—
a blackbird strolls down
the clay tile walk

I had composed less accomplished sequences before this one, and since then I have composed and published more accomplished ones, particularly those inspired by vacations to exotic places. But as a haiku exercise, writing sequences is quite satisfying.

CONCLUSION

To sum up, you should remember that a haiku is a moment of insight connected with nature. Most often in such a haiku two images are linked in three short-long-short horizontal lines of eight to twelve words. You are not writing lyric poetry when you write haiku, so avoid "poetic" expressions like metaphor. Also, don't explain anything, your images contain feelings that your reader will respond to in and of themselves. Above all, relax and be open to the experience of nature. Those things in nature that touch you will become your haiku. And those haiku will touch others.

There is something important in every haiku. A haiku is your moment, and you express it for an important reason. Although you may need to develop your sense of focus and polish in expressing haiku, as you would with any art form, all a haiku often needs is a little tighter focus and a little polish. What is important in haiku, however, is that moment of insight when you feel in some way connected with the natural world and you desire to share this insight with others.

Telling a Joke: Senryu

WE HAVE SEEN THAT HAIKU, for the most part, offers deep insight into nature even if it includes subjects taken from everyday activities. We have also seen that haiku can sometimes be amusing. But there is a kind of poetry that is similar in form to haiku but deals exclusively with human nature and most often is expressed as a joke. This form is called senryu.

Take a look again at Tom Tico's Christmas haiku and another poem on the same subject:

Christmas Eve . . .
   at the lot, the trees
     not chosen

      —Tom Tico

Christmas eve—
the clerk cuts
the tree's price

      —Peggy Heinrich

Both poems more or less have the three-line short-long-short form with a definite punctuation break at the end of the first line. Both, in fact, have almost the same first line. But look at the punctuation. The three dots of the ellipsis in the first haiku are setting the mood by stretching out the familiar Christmas scene. We are allowed to imagine all the things we associate with Christmas Eve. The dash in the second haiku is making a clear break. It is simply telling us when this poem took place. As we see, both are about a Christmas tree lot. We have all seen these lots with trees leaning against each other under strings of bright lights. However, Tom Tico's haiku is about the loneliness of the scene of the unsold trees left in the lot. This haiku has human feeling attached to it, but it is really about the loneliness of the scene and the deep feeling that scene evokes in us. In the second we know we are looking at a joke about human nature. The clerk will not be able to sell his trees after this night. We know what happens to the sold ones a week after Christmas. The clerk is therefore a little desperate. So for this last-minute customer he lowers the tree's price. The clerk is interested in both a sale and a profit. But on this night, when we are supposed to have goodwill, the clerk's act could be vaguely understood as a kindness, which it isn't. We can all see at least one joke on human nature in this little drama. Heinrich's poem, which won second place in the humor category of the 1999 Hawaii Education Association Annual International Haiku Contest, is therefore a senryu. Here the poem is not centered on natural images that provoke deep feelings, as in haiku, but on these little human dramas that take the form of a joke.

This is not to say that there is a hard-and-fast line between poems about nature and poems about human nature. A poem such as the following takes place in nature, and the joke on the narrator is due to nature. Is it a haiku or a senryu? You be the judge:

> my tracks . . . their tracks . . .
> suddenly face to face
> with returning geese
>
> —Leatrice Lifshitz

In general, a poem with deep feelings centered on nature or on human associations with the seasons is a haiku, and a poem with a humorous perspective on the failings and weaknesses of human nature is a senryu, even though a serious poem about deep human feeling in which the natural world takes no part seems like a haiku.

CLASSICAL JAPANESE SENRYU

Nonetheless, some of the earliest Japanese senryu writers, and many modern ones, would consider such a poem about deep human feeling a senryu, and some of the earliest Japanese senryu writers would consider humanlike gestures in the natural world a senryu. Here are two such examples of early Japanese senryu:

lost child found—
the father gives thanks
in a hoarse voice

the chicken wants
to tell us something:
fidgeting its feet

Both of these senryu were published anonymously, but this is no longer the practice in Japan. Senryu were a type of comic poetry that developed in the eighteenth century when the feudal system of warlords and samurai gave way to the expansion of merchant-class values and the growth of cities. Senryu, which were named after a judge of comic verse contests, Karai Senryū, sounded like jokes about what it was like living in such times in the city. Perhaps the most amusing senryu were on professional corruption such as this one:

the official's child—
how well he learns to open
and close his fist!

We can see how this child has learned to imitate his father's hand reaching out for a bribe. Or at least it seems so to the senryu's author. You can see a kind of wordplay here. The young child is learning how to grasp things with his hand like all children do. But because he is the son of an official who, like other officials of the time, takes bribes, the child's natural gesture becomes a satire on the father and all officials in general. Sometimes these senryu were lively, sometimes witty, and sometimes even vulgar:

now that he has a child	Zen priest,
he knows all the names	his meditation finished
of the local dogs	he looks for fleas

The first is a touching observation of family life while the second is a satire on the all-too-human nature of a kind of priest known for their enlightenment. The following examples show how lively and down-to-earth senryu can be:

one bite	I stopped to urinate—
and I am jumping around—	and missed
red peppers	the ferry

Notice how these two senryu are like a little scene from a slapstick comedy in which crude actions are presented in a loud or noisy manner, or in the more toned-down way of situation comedies on television or at the movies. It is in this form that thousands and thousands of Japanese write today, often in the manner of "serious senryu" or outright satire like that found in the eighteenth-century senryu, which has adapted itself well to the modern American scene.

MODERN AMERICAN SENRYU

Two of my favorite American senryu are by two of the best practitioners of the form, and each of the senryu has a very modern focus:

Hole in the ozone	side by side
my bald spot . . .	his and her
sunburned	computers
—Garry Gay	—Tom Clausen

How could we make fun of such a serious subject as the hole in the ozone layer, which could possibly have horrible effects on human beings and the environment, such as depressed immune levels and even cancer among human beings and animals? There is not much hard evidence for these things so far, and many people think of the "hole in the ozone" as some vague idea associated with changes in the environment. Garry Gay's senryu has particularized this vague term. And he has done it through humor by comparing the picture we have in our heads of an open space among the clouds to the bald spot on his head. That spot is sunburned, making the idea of the hole in the ozone concrete. There is something amusing in taking a fuzzy idea and illustrating it with a very down-to-earth, even amusing, example. The second senryu, which won first place in the humor category of the 1999 Hawaii Education Association Annual International Haiku Contest, also addresses a modern topic in an amusing way. Many of us are familiar with the way couples use his and her towels, outfits, and bicycles to express their togetherness. The computer is a fairly recent technical tool, yet we find it everywhere. It is also taking on more and more significance as a communication tool. The humor in this haiku comes from adding the computer, something we think of as simply a machine, to the list of "his and her" items. But since the computer is a communication device that connects people regardless of the distance, there is added humor here. These computers are next to each other. If the couple are both using the computers, even if they are talking to each other, they are primarily processing information or communicating with someone else. This complexity of communication, when it is placed in the context of the "his and her" bond, is simply amusing. Notice how the last line is a surprise punch line that makes the senryu into a joke. And notice similarly how in Garry Gay's senryu the humorous jokelike comparison in lines one or two have a kind of punch line in the additional humor of line three.

SENRYU BY CHILDREN

At that Japanese spring festival I attended in 1999, a very young girl came up to the Burlington Haiku Group work table with her mother. She sat down, willing to try to write a haiku. We talked for a while about her experiences at the festival, where one of the most dramatic events was the presentation by a group of *taiko* drummers. Taiko drumming includes beating aggressively on drums of all sizes. The drummers whirl around and shout. Most of the rhythms of the pieces are extremely fast, the physical beating movements very rapid. The event as a whole is quite lively and conveys a happy and cheerful mood, but the sound is thundering. The young girl told me about how she enjoyed the drumming and wrote this senryu:

> Japanese festival
> I put my fingers in my ears
> for the taiko drumming

Anyone who has heard the booming sound of these drums will be amused by this senryu. When we consider that most of the Japanese arts displayed at a festival like this are quiet and delicate in nature—paper folding, flower arranging, calligraphy, haiku writing—you can see an added humor in the comparison.

WABI—THE BEAUTY OF ORDINARY THINGS

One of the main characteristics of senryu is the liveliness it finds in its subjects. There is an obvious liveliness in nature that may be associated with the idea of wabi, the beauty of ordinary things. Wabi responds to the depth of stillness, or sabi, in a haiku with liveliness. It captures the day-to-day presence of ordinary things and exhibits the vitality that lies beneath their surfaces. Here is the source of earthly humor and comedy, for there is something joyful in this vitality, like the geese in Leatrice Lifshitz's poem or the neglected garden growing faster than ever in Molly Magner's haiku, which we saw earlier. Such liveliness in nature translates into the clamor of everyday human activities in senryu. Look for such energy and play in American senryu. For example, I was visiting Miami, Florida, in the winter of 1998. South Miami is noted for its restaurants and nightlife, and I wanted to see it for myself. The active part of this area is a long strip of restaurants, block after block, that is separated from the ocean by a long, narrow grassy park. One night I walked along this strip. There were outdoor cafés, restaurants displaying their special dishes on tables on the sidewalk, brightly lit arcades selling who knows what, and an overall atmosphere of high energy and excitement. There was barely room to walk because of all the people. But most of us were drawn to the loud music near the northern end of the strip. A small stage projected out onto the sidewalk. On it a man was playing incredibly intense music on his guitar while his female companion vigorously danced beside him. I even recognized one of the songs, which was based on a Central European folk melody. The crowd extended halfway down each side of the restaurant and onto the street and into the park. When a car wanted to get by, the crowd opened up for a moment. Everyone was entranced by the music. I was standing on the curbstone just in front of the park, directly across from the stage. Because of the mass of people I couldn't get any closer. I noticed that many people were dancing in the little space they had. And then I looked to my left and there in the street I saw this:

> South Miami night—
> a man with a wooden walker dances
> to gypsy music

I was, of course, not making fun of the man. I was celebrating the liveliness he embodied there, dancing in that lively scene with his female companion dancing next to him.

SATIRE IN SENRYU

The other main characteristic of senryu is satire. Every culture likes to poke fun at the weaknesses they see in human nature. We have all enjoyed, at one time or another, comic strips, political cartoons, and situation comedies. We have heard the expression "boys will be boys," which somehow tries to forgive the lapses in our actions. But there is something funny in having a comedian point out the inconsistencies in a public figure or an ordinary person. We are not so much offended as amused by having the now-so-obvious truth revealed to us. We saw how early Japanese senryu satirized officials and their corruption and even the all-too-human activities of a Zen priest. Take a look at the satire in this modern American senryu:

> California friends—
> here today
> gone today.
>
> —Alexis Rotella

I once saw a cartoon in *The New Yorker* magazine. The same drawing appeared twice. In each panel one man was talking to another man. He was saying something but his thoughts were written in a balloon above his head as they are in many cartoons. Under the left panel were the words EAST COAST. The man was saying something like "Who cares!" to the man, only worse, but he was thinking, "Have a nice day!" Under the right panel were the words WEST COAST. This time the man was saying "Have a nice day!" but he was thinking "Who cares!"—only worse. The West Coast, and particularly California, has a reputation for its fast pace and insincerity. Alexis Rotella is offering us a satiric commentary on this reputation. She is also making a pun, or a play on words. We may know the old expression, "Here today, gone tomorrow." It is meant to be a comment on how really short a human life span is. This senryu gives us a miniature concrete example of this wise saying. But because of its context, which makes the situation less serious and even absurd, we are amused.

FORMS OF SENRYU

Joke

A senryu may take many forms. One of the most obvious, and one that may incorporate all of senryu's other forms, is the joke. A stand-up comedian tells a joke and we laugh. What that comedian is doing is telling a funny story. What a senryu is often doing is telling a very short funny story. I was staying in the city of Boston for one month and was determined to use the subway system, or "T," whenever I could. I had a subway map, and it looked simple. There were four subway lines: red, orange, green, and blue. Each of the four lines was almost straight and intersected with two of the other lines in two station stops. I couldn't have a problem with this system. However, when I actually got on the subway and tried to go across town using more than one line, I had a surprise:

> Boston "T":
> a more complicated map
> at every transfer

Of course the joke was on me, and this little story serves as an example of how simple things can get more and more complex.

Another aspect of senryu is the punch line or the amusing point of a story that usually comes in the last line of the senryu. A comedian saves the punch line of his joke for the joke's end because our surprise will add to the humor and the enjoyment we have in the joke. Look at this senryu:

> so many favorites
> on this new display—
> Banned Book Week
>
> —Charles Rossiter

We are prepared to wonder what nice thing is being displayed. The punch line undermines our expectations and makes us laugh for having been caught with our guard down.

Wordplay

We have seen that wordplay can be incorporated into a senryu, like the pun in Alexis Rotella's satire on California. Here is a senryu that uses the pun, like so many modern American senryu, as the main feature of its joke:

> freeway begins—with a toll booth
>
> —Donald McLeod

The pun is direct: something "free" becomes something that has a "toll." But the delight we take in this senryu is from how it uncovers for us an aspect of the word *freeway* that we may never have thought of.

Other wordplay in senryu may include two levels of wordplay, as in this one:

> a new face on TV—
> the regular weatherman
> under the weather
>
> —Michael Dylan Welch

We all know the expression "to be under the weather," which means to be sick. It is almost a cliché, an overused word or phrase. It probably originally meant that someone became ill because of bad weather. But by applying this phrase to someone who is an expert on weather, the phrase comes alive in an amusing way. And we also might be amused because, unconsciously, we might wonder why someone who is an expert on the weather could be "under the weather."

Found Senryu

A final form of senryu is a type of found poem. We might be amused by what we read on a vanity license plate, in the wording of an advertisement, or in the relationship between what someone says and what they are doing. But many found senryu are based on store signs, as in this one:

> in front of
> the burned-out restaurant
> REAL PIT BARBEQUE
>
> —Kenneth C. Leibman

The author came upon this scene, perhaps seeing the sign first and then noticing the remains of the restaurant, which may have been reduced to charcoal. In fact, the restaurant may have looked very much like the barbecue pit it advertised. Or so we might imagine.

SUBJECT MATTER OF SENRYU

Satire

Apart from the basic form of the joke and the use of wordplay, senryu has three distinct kinds of content. The first and most general is satire. As we have seen, satire exposes shortcomings in human behavior. It uses wit, or a keenness of observation, and irony, or a contrast between two things, to make fun of human folly, vice, and basic stupidity in order to bring these things to light. Take a look at the satire in the following senryu.

> ginkgo biloba
> forgetting where
> I put it
>
> —R. A. Stefanac

> our director espouses
> more expansive ideals
> . . . I stretch
>
> —Tom Clausen

tourist town
postcards of the waterfall
racked upside down

—John Stevenson

Each senryu is exposing some phony aspect of a recognizable situation in our culture. In the first, which won an Honorable Mention in the humor category of the 1999 Hawaii Education Association Annual Haiku Contest, the humor comes as much from a critical view of natural remedies as it does from the obvious play on the medicine itself. Ginkgo biloba is said to help increase a person's mental sharpness. The joke here is that the medicine doesn't work. Television advertisements for this product assure the viewer that their ability to remember things will increase when they take it. You cannot help but feel that the author is poking fun at such a claim in this senryu. We are all aware of situations in which the head of an organization to which we belong seems overly fond of his or her own words. The level of language represented by the last word of the first line and the second word in the second line of Tom Clausen's senryu present such a person's words. The last line lets the hot air out of these overly pretentious words with a physical pun on the word *expansive*. Many of us have gone to places that are considered "tourist traps" and many of us have avoided such places. The waterfall that is the attraction in the last senryu might even be the magnificent Niagara Falls. Nonetheless, the true nature of tourist towns, which is not about the beauty of the waterfall, is revealed in the upside-down postcards.

Human Nature

The second major kind of content in senryu is an amusing observation on the weaknesses of human behavior. Look at these examples of classic Japanese senryu:

until the rain stops
he argues over the price
of an umbrella

"Don't let this worry you!"
and then he tells you something
that really worries you

We are often in serious situations and have to become creative to get ourselves out of them. Human beings are resourceful, and there is something amusing about how they get themselves out of trouble. The man in the first senryu is caught in a rainstorm. He doesn't want to get wet so he goes into an umbrella shop. He may not really want to buy the umbrella. He certainly tries to lower its price. But once the rain stops it doesn't matter anymore. It is the unexpected outcome of this observed scene that makes the senryu humorous. We might know someone like the person described in the second senryu. Certainly some American senryu writers do:

"I don't mean
    to interrupt," she says,
        again.

—Alexis Rotella

"I can't stay!"
    she takes an hour
    to tell me why

—Yvonne Hardenbrook

Notice the amusing implications, in the following senryu, on the overly ambitious imagination some people have from time to time:

at the sushi bar
noticing the goldfish bowl—
empty today

—Donnie Nichols

Many of us have seen fish tanks in oriental restaurants and enjoyed the color and movement of the fish while we waited for our food. Many of us may know that sushi is a Japanese dish that combines raw fish with rice. Some of us may have even eaten sushi and liked it. The author of this senryu is perhaps not so seriously imagining that the usually displayed goldfish wound up as sushi!

Vulgarity

The final major kind of content, more acceptable in eighteenth-century Japan than it is today, is vulgar or risqué words or situations, ones that are commonly thought to be indecent or obscene, while at the same time amusing to some. Here is an example from classical Japanese senryu and a modern American one:

a horse passes gas:
four or five people suffer
on the ferry boat

signing
the deaf boy shows me
how to swear

—Christopher Suarez

The poor souls on the ferry boat are caught unawares and suffer. And if the boat is small and crowded, as it might be, there would unfortunately be no escape for them. We might laugh at this situation, but we are taught not to be amused or make fun of the suffering or even of differences in others. Christopher Suarez is not making fun of the hearing-impaired boy. In fact, he seems delighted to learn that this boy knows how to swear. But of course human nature is human nature, and this comes out in the senryu. We are also taught to "watch our language" and not use obscene words. It is amusing that this lively boy would share his impishness with the author of this senryu and teach him how to curse in sign language.

THEMES

Relationships

There are many themes taken up by modern American senryu writers, but some of the most common ones are relationships, professions, pets, children, and the modern world. It is interesting to note that these themes were also common in the then modern Golden Age of Japanese eighteenth-century senryu.

Unfortunately, there always seems to be some kind of conflict in our relationships. The trick is to find something funny in such conflict. And this is precisely what senryu does:

channel dispute
she aims the clicker
at me

—Dee Evetts

deep in the argument
even her stomach
growling at me

—John Sheirer

Many of us have had disagreements about which television channel we should watch. But who would see the humor in the situation in the first haiku? Could anyone imagine, like Dee Evetts, his companion being able to turn him off or change what he is saying as if he were a television? The second senryu is based on a pun on the word *growling*. Of course the author's companion's stomach is not growling at him. For that matter, his companion is probably not growling at him at all. But the pun allows John Sheirer to make fun of the conflict, whatever it is. An added bit of humor here is that in reality the conflict is momentarily interrupted by the growling stomach, thereby reducing its seriousness and reminding the two companions that there are other things in life besides this argument.

Professional Satire

Satires on professional people produced some of the most amusing classical Japanese senryu. One device used in these senryu is a kind of conceptual pun in which there is a play on a person's profession or appearance. Here we find a ladder salesman escaping to a roof and a chinaware seller whose "business crashes." Take a look at these two American versions of such punning:

Weight lifter
slowly lifting
the tea cup

—Garry Gay

at his favorite deli
the bald man finds a hair
in his soup

—Michael Dylan Welch

The incongruity between the weight lifter's physique and how delicately he drinks his tea takes advantage of the visual pun in the
repeated word *lift,* while the obvious incongruity of a bald man finding
a hair in his soup naturally produces the humor in the second senryu.
But we also might be amused by the fact that for once a diner in a
restaurant can be absolutely sure that it is not *his* hair in the soup. A
more subtler version of this kind of senryu is the following:

dermatologist's office
on the bare white walls
a diagram of acne

—Robert Epstein

The author is in the skin specialist's office for some reason. The visual
pun here is that the picture of acne on the pure white wall reminds us
of the real acne that sometimes appears on the unblemished skin of
someone's face. And if someone, even the author, is being treated for
acne, he or she would be made to feel a bit more self-conscious about
his or her appearance. The absurdity of that overly dramatic situation
would add another dimension of humor to this senryu.

But by far, most senryu expose the corruption and phoniness that is
often found in those who practice the professions. Take a look at a
classical Japanese senryu about a person who arranges marriages and
three modern American senryu about plumbers, French waiters, and
politicians:

"She may only have one eye
but it is a pretty one,"
says the matchmaker

when the owner comes
the plumbers start talking Greek
to each other

—L. A. Davidson

French waiter
his accent heavier at dinner
than at lunch

—Yvonne Hardenbrook

She's running for office—
for the first time
my neighbor waves.

—Alexis Rotella

The classical example might seem in poor taste today, but we can imagine the deceitful matchmaker trying desperately to earn his commission. Many people feel that those who make repairs on our houses or cars are also deceitful, and trying to hide something from them. L. A. Davidson presents us with just such a situation. And her senryu's humor might just benefit from the subtle play on the phrase "It's Greek to me!" which means you can't understand something. The French waiter is not trying to hide something but to overdo his manner in order to get a bigger tip to go with the bigger dinner bill. Alexis Rotella's neighbor also exhibits a kind of phoniness that we recognize in public personalities, especially politicians. All of the situations depicted here could have been, with a little adjustment, lifted from a television situation comedy like *Frasier*.

Pets

Another common theme is the pets that share our lives and become part of the family. Two senryu examples show us exactly how a pet can be as playful and as endearing as a child:

while I'm gone
my dog
takes the driver's seat

—Christopher Herold

yard sale
pet dog's price tag:
$50,000

—Francine Porad

We have all seen dogs left in a car when their owners have gone into a shop. These dogs usually sit in the passenger seat and stare out the window or straight ahead. If you get too close to the car some of them will bark at you. This dog is different. It has learned from its master, and if it could, it would share some of the driving with him. The amusing absurdity of this thought is similar to that of the price tag and the price tag's amount on the pet dog in the second senryu. In other words, its owners are advertising just how much they care for their dog.

Children

In classical Japanese senryu children are treated with tender regard, but in modern American senryu there is an interest in the amusing things children do. You may have seen the TV program *Kids Say the Darndest Things*. The two senryu examples for this theme illustrate the truth of that show's title:

last grandchild
asks if she remembers
the dinosaurs

—Dee Evetts

fake cell phone—
the toddler on his porch
striding back and forth

—Carol Montgomery

To very young children, old is old. So, to them, an old grandmother could be as old as a dinosaur. And, unfortunately, sometimes when they are angry at someone, they might call them an old dinosaur. The adult author of this senryu may have thought that this made his senryu all the more silly. The second senryu is also silly. Like pets who can mimic their masters, children sometimes copy the mannerisms of the adults around them. Seen positively, this is how children learn how to act properly. Seen in another way, such mimicry can be inappropriate and absurd. That toy companies make cell phones for children may seem amusing to some. But the way the toddler is moving reminds us how some adults, when in a serious conversation on their cell phone, pace back and forth. This toddler is having an imaginary conversation on a phony telephone, yet his movements make him look like one of these adults!

The Modern World

The cell phone in this haiku leads us to a final theme in modern American senryu: the modern world. We have looked at senryu about the hole in the ozone, computers, fast-paced contemporary California culture, and designer natural medicine. Such a world, which seems to move so quickly and surrounds us with newer and newer technology, needs the humor of senryu to put things in perspective. Take a look at these last two examples that respond with humor to this world:

worrying
that the stress workshop
will be crowded

—David Carlson

the secret world
of my journal
X-rayed at the airport

—Molly McGee

The first senryu is a witty comment on the stress that many of us feel in our lives. Stress is in fact a serious national health concern. But even when the author of this senryu attempts to take part in a preventative medicine workshop, he is so overwhelmed by stress that he can only think of a stressful possibility in that workshop. The absurdity of thinking about a stress-reducing workshop in terms of more stress is humorous. A journal or a diary is a private record. No one wants someone to look at his or her journal or diary without permission. Yet here not a person but a machine is in a manner of speaking "reading" the author's journal. The joke is a pun on this kind of "reading" by the X-ray machine. For of course even if the journal is X-rayed or "read" by the machine, its private writings are not understood. And there may be another pun on the word *X-ray*, which sounds like X-rated. The secrets in our journals may not be X-rated, but they will be highly personal. The hint of this comparison makes this senryu even more amusing. And nowhere but in the modern world of airport X-rays and stressed-out stress workshops can we find just this kind of humor to help us create a sense of proportion for these things.

CONCLUSION

So, to sum up, my advice for writing senryu is to have a good sense of humor and to keep your eye open for the funny things people do.

Telling a Story: Haibun

IF A HAIKU IS AN INSIGHT into a moment of experience, a haibun is the story or narrative of how someone came to have that insight.

A haibun is a prose narrative that is autobiographical—that is, in haibun you are telling a story about something you did or saw. Prose is ordinary writing, as opposed to poetry. Haibun is prose writing that is expressed poetically, with figures of speech and rhythmic sound values, and is full of emotion, like the writing in a diary. What is unusual about haibun is that it includes haiku. The haiku will act like little punctuation marks of feeling in the prose. Sometimes the haiku will illustrate the insight of your narrative, and sometimes it will extend the implications of your narrative. So, in a haibun, someone tells a story full of emotion that leads us to an insight about oneself, another person, a place, or a thing, and this is emphasized through one or more haiku. In haibun the reader is moved by the interrelationship between the prose writing and the haiku.

CLASSICAL JAPANESE HAIBUN

From an early period, with travel diaries from at least the tenth century, Japanese writers were incorporating poetry into their prose writing. In fact, the world's first novel, the eleventh-century *The Tale of Genji*, does this. But in Japan, haibun is commonly associated with personal diaries and travel journals (although it is not much practiced today). In these we find short records of an event expressed with poetic feeling and concluded with a haiku. Two of the most well-known are Bashō's *Narrow Path to the Interior*, a record of his long journey to the remote regions of northern Japan at the end of the seventeenth century, and Issa's *My Spring*, a diary of the events in his life and his village at the beginning of the nineteenth century. Here are two examples from Bashō, a playful one about a snowball and the other the narrative of the cricket haiku we have already discussed, which is from *Narrow Path to the Interior*. Again, notice how each haibun creates a mood through its prose and how the concluding haiku relates to these moods:

SNOWBALL

That disciple Sora has temporarily taken up residence nearby, and we visit each other mornings and evenings. When I'm preparing my meal, he helps by adding firewood, and when I'm boiling tea, he arrives at my door. He's a man who prefers to live alone, and our relationship is pure and strong. One night he visited me after a snowfall:

> you build up the fire,
> and I'll show you something nice:
> a big snowball!

THE MOUNTAIN TEMPLE

There is a temple called Ryūshakuji in the province of Yamagata. It was built by the great priest Jikaku and is noted for its absolute tranquillity. Since many people advised me to see it, I changed my course from Obanazawa, though the temple was seven miles or more away. It was still light when I reached it. I arranged lodging with the priests at the foot of the mountain and climbed to the temple on the mountaintop. The whole mountain was made up of massive boulders thrown together and ancient pines and oaks, and the rocky ground was covered with old velvety moss. The doors of all the shrines were closed and there was not a single sound. But I scrambled over the rocks and bowed reverently before each shrine. I felt the profound spiritual power of this place pervading my heart.

> stillness:
> sinking into the rocks
> a cricket's voice

The prose of these haibun may seem a little flat in comparison to modern American haibun. But remember that these are translations from Japanese; they would be more rhythmic in the original language. They look similar to many modern American haibun in form. A short paragraph followed by one haiku is in fact the most common form of haibun written in English. Like the American haibun, Bashō's sustains a particular mood. Both of Bashō's concluding haiku, like many modern American concluding haiku, sum up the mood of the prose, although the first one ends in a playful joke. It is Bashō's second haibun, with its more serious tone, that many American haibun writers seem to prefer, although some do write haibun in the lighter, playful tone of "Snowball," which included a conversational phrase like the lighthearted scolding phrase "that disciple Sora." If anything, your own haibun should not sound wooden or plodding with merely flat description. You should heat up your prose with rhythm and sound values as well as figurative expressions to put across your emotion. Notice how Bashō is trying to get Sora to loosen up. The scolding phrase leads us to the prank in the last line of the haiku in "Snowball" just as the "I do this / he does that" repeated sentence structure leads to lines one and two of the haiku. The more serious "The Mountain Temple" builds its mood of stillness by touching images of the setting that create an atmosphere of starkness, age, and stillness. The haiku subtly connects its feeling to the prose not simply by intensifying the atmosphere of stillness but by comparing the cricket's song being "soaked up" by the stillness of the rocks to the peace and stillness of the place entering and taking over Bashō's deepest self.

American versions of haibun began in the late 1950s with travel diaries by the poet Gary Snyder and fiction by the novelist Jack Kerouac. In the mid-1960s, haibun began to appear in American haiku journals. From the seventies through the nineties the typical haibun was a one-paragraph nature sketch followed by a haiku. However, there has also been much experimentation with haibun, including book-length travel journals, many-sectioned autobiographical accounts, and nontraditional fiction. American haibun has also shied away from the common delicate, understated style of classical Japanese haibun, although some haibun writers do use this style. American haibun, by incorporating some of that delicacy, also represents some of the strongest writing directed toward our deep connection with nature and the inner workings of our own humanity. For example, consider this award-winning haibun, included in the anthology *Wedge of Light*, which presented haibun chosen from the first ever haibun contest in English in the late 1990s:

A GARDEN BOUQUET

Dwarfed by sunflowers ten feet tall, I reach through a spray of lacy cosmos to cut a full-bloomed pink dahlia. Adding one more to my almost full basket, brimming with yellow and red zinnias, blue bachelor's buttons and black-eyed susans. Before leaving, I spot a red tomato for tonight's dinner.

> an applesauce jar
> carefully chosen flowers
> one small ladybug

Balanced between my knees, trying not to spill water, we drive to the cemetery in silence.

—Sally Secor

This wonderful haibun is delicate and understated. The ordinariness of the applesauce jar used as a flower vase and the naturalness of having a ladybug on one of the just-cut flowers little prepares us for where the flowers are going. Because of the tomato picked for dinner we assume that the flowers are to accompany that dinner. But we are mistaken. Yet we are made to see in some elusive way, perhaps on a second reading of this haibun, that there is something natural about this gift of flowers and an unintentional ladybug that somehow relieves our anxiety about a visit to a cemetery. Again, we learn something about the natural patterns in our lives and in nature.

FORMS OF AMERICAN HAIBUN

American haibun can take many forms but four of the major ones are: a nature sketch, a travel journal, an autobiographical account, and fiction.

The Nature Sketch

The nature sketch is by far the most common subject for a haibun. In it we are really trying to learn something about nature and something about ourselves through a deep or delicate connection with some aspect of nature:

STRANDS

The nest has been rescued from the tree surgeon's pruning. It is oval. It is empty. Such a small but wonderful achievement! No hands, just beak and feet, and yet the bird has made its nest strong, though light. It has held life, and contributed to the cycle of a bird life.

> fledglings have flown;
> late sunlight highlights
> a few tawny strands

> —Emily Romano

Here, the bird's nest, come upon by chance, is seen up close to be a miraculous achievement. It becomes a living example of the cycle of life in nature. The sunlit strands in the haiku become a metaphor or representation of the two or three young birds that were born and raised in this nest and have some time ago flown away. It is late in the day, perhaps nearing sunset. The moodiness of this time of day intensifies the delicacy of the expressed feeling for the absent birds and for the ways of nature.

The Travel Journal

A travel journal allows us to remember things we have observed and enjoyed on a trip. We all have a story about some vacation we had, whether about some beautiful thing we saw, some unusual person we met, or some incredible experience we had. Travel journal haibun reduce these experiences to short, well-crafted accounts that emphasize our emotion and lead us to a realization. Here is one about a well-known Native American site in the Southwest that once was alive with a now long-vanished culture:

CHACO CANYON HAIBUN

There is a petroglyph on a small cliff in the desert about one and a half miles from the road. On cream-colored sandstone is a deep red painting of a star, a crescent moon, and the sun. It is thought to be a picture of the supernova of 1054. The rocks, sand, and scraggly bushes are just about the same as nine hundred years ago. I stand alone in this vast expanse of desert and imagine an Anasazi Indian carefully painting the picture to record the fantastic event he had or she had witnessed. Now, through this painting, here on the desert cliff, I can share that person's wonder of the cosmic forces that shape the universe and together across the centuries we marvel at the mystery.

distant starlight
falling on age-old rocks
my hand casts a shadow

—Michael Ketchek

This haibun perfectly reflects its author's communion with the ancient artist's wonder. The miraculousness of this sharing is underscored in the prose by emphasizing how long ago the painting was made and in the haiku by how far away the stars are and the age of the rocks upon which the painting was drawn. Such age and such distance heighten the emotional coloring of the closeness the author feels toward the artist.

Autobiographical Account

An autobiographical account about some revelation we find in daily life can make a powerful haibun. Here is one of my own that compresses a day's events and memories of past events within an overriding emotion:

AGLOW

For some time now the late November days have been bleak. Once or twice there have been moments of brightening. To cheer myself I had gone last night to see *The Secret Garden* and recalled Keats's "magic casements" for some reason, enchanted as I was with memories of when as a child my father took me to see the animated version of *Alice in Wonderland*. We had walked in after the film had begun. It was one of my first trips to the movies. What I remember is entering a sacred special place. The dark theater demanding a sense of awe. And there at the end of the tunnel of darkness the magical animated figures in brilliant pastel colors—a figuration from another dimension. Of dream. Of spirit. And the breathless rising shots last night in *The Secret Garden* of a diminishing wild landscape covered with the moving of shadows of clouds in bright light.

So I jogged my ritual run this morning in Durand Eastman Park in the drizzle:

> November drizzle—
> the squirrel's head beneath
> the wet leaves

and drove back home in the, now, light rain:

> November rain—
> the outdoor jack-o'-lantern
> collapsing on itself

In the afternoon I went to a bookstore for the signing of my anthology *Haiku Moment*. The sales were fair but I had a good time (the manager said that she would have no trouble selling the remaining copies during the holiday season). On the way home on the expressway my attention suddenly was drawn to a haze of flame at the horizon. The late afternoon light was collected in the top of the stand of naked trees on the horizon. I was somehow transported to some other dimension. I remembered the smile I had when I left *The Secret Garden* last night. I was, in some intangible way, home:

> late afternoon light—
> the stand of bare trees aglow
> on the horizon

In some mysterious way, memories of my childhood provoked a transformation in my state of undefined moodiness. This in turn allowed me a general openness to experience that connected me to a revelation of the natural world in a kind of purity untouched by the worldly wise adult I thought I had become. This is an example of an epiphany, an occasion of deep spiritual revelation, that the haibun form, in its best examples, can express as a record of elevating and inspiring moments in our lives.

Fiction

A haibun can also take the form of pure made-up fiction. Here the emotion of the haibun does not come directly from our lived experience but from made-up characters and situations. The early-twentieth-century Japanese novelist Natsume Soseki wrote poetically expressed novels that incorporated haiku, such as *The Three-Cornered Hat*. Jack Kerouac wrote similar novels, but his were very much based on his own experiences. As a more recent example, here is a chapter from *Half Hidden by Twilight*, one of a trilogy of novels by D. S. Lliteras:

IDIOT

I did not like driving for pleasure. But I did not feel like going back to the apartment.

I did not want to engage in any human contact. So, I took a right and a left and traveled into this and that direction for a short while.

I did not want to explore the consequences of existence: I was spiritually exhausted. But I glanced at the brown rug lying on the back seat and saw one person's need. Then I saw the demise of all people: the same thing happening to the many—making us one, long before the disappearance of the one.

I made a right and a left followed by another left. I had had enough. I was hungry and probably in love and I was squandering this precious moment with metaphysical introspection.

"Drive, you idiot. It's a beautiful day, can't you see?"

clearly winter
through bare branches
the sky

The narrator in this chapter, just as I was in the preceding haibun, is in a moody, emotionally disoriented state, perhaps even depressed. But here the narrator is intellectually trying to work out some greater scheme to account for how things are. The chapter, however, becomes a kind of joke with the quoted words in the last line of the prose. It is saying in so many words, "Forget your speculation. Look at what's right in front of your nose. It's all so obvious!" The haiku presents us with what the narrator sees. In many ways this chapter is a narrative of what Zen Buddhism would call an awakening: to see things just as they are without any mental preconceptions. But you would have to read the novel from which this chapter came in order to see if the narrator truly became enlightened.

Nature Haibun

The purpose of writing nature haibun is to gain some insight into the world of nature and to make ourselves larger through the beauty, wisdom, and grace we find there. Notice how effortlessly the following three examples exhibit a perfect union of the narrator's feeling and the often overwhelmingly stirring moods of nature. As in nature haiku, one has to still oneself to see and experience the subtlety of such beauty. Notice the figurative language used to describe the night and the wind in the following haibun:

WINTER HAIBUN

The crisp, predawn air buoys me across a field shimmering with rime. Just inside the edge of the woods I sit on a moldering log. Nearby a sapling leans toward the first saffron stains of the new day. It is torn and scraped. When the sap rises it will die.

Night slowly comes apart, dissolves into pools of purple. Lavender washes the mottled bark of the near pines.

They begin as a whisper out across the crown of the forest. Now they hum a lullaby, now mimic a far-off freight. They toy with my senses, rise, fall, undulate along uncharted paths. They search to my left, now to my right. The scattered elements gather, intensify, relinquish all their secrets. The train rushes full at me.

> midwinter—
> dawn winds approach
> the buck's rubbing tree

> —Hal Roth

See how elegantly the author has captured the feel of daybreak in a stark winter woods by centering his description on the young tree that will die because of the wounds made by the antlers of a male deer. The poetic description of the wind helps to support the overall mood of harsh desolation.

Contrast this haibun with the following, in which man and nature are more warmly integrated:

THE ORDER OF STARS

All summer long I share this river with the various migrant species that come to shelter and feed in its bounteous arms: Canada geese and sandhill cranes, upland beavers and lowland muskrat, fleet trout and wallowing carp; and, most seasonally, other human beings as well. With them I exchange small talk about crops and crappies, great blues and boats, the weather and the World Series. For a few months the most notable objects on the water are bright-colored fiberglass craft powered by noisy engines churning through the steady clear currents. Along the shore, silver trailers with out-of-

state plates and mud-spattered pickups beside orange tents pop up
in the flood plain. Smoky fires and loud talk ride the wind.

> calm evening
> the ballgame comes play-by-play
> across the water

When autumn appears, and the waters cool, first weekdays, then
all days, find the river devoid of men. It is at this time, when the
river and I are alone, that I am most able to come to my senses,
become most truly human. It is not that I do not enjoy the company
of my fellow men. But their presence illustrates to me what a man
is, while in their absence I am permitted to think on what a man can
be, and to represent him well here among the wild and untutored,
where there is no preference for things human. I am most able to
shed the veneer of humanity and simply be, a human animal
amongst these other animals, a presence amidst their presences.

It is now, when the river is barren, that I am most forcibly
struck by the solitariness of wild animals. How rare it is to see
animals in the company of a species not their own. Bears do not
traffic with deer, beavers give the muskrats a wide berth, and chipmunks dart away at the approach of a hare. Only the birds are
excepted: upon the waters, intermingled, I espy mallards keeping
company with Canada geese; the cranes and herons share the
shingled bank; and the strong straight flights of the kingfisher are
looped together by the barn swallows' arabesques.

The dog is happy enough on its own, quite apart from these
deliberations. He races about for sheer joy, biting at the white
water of the rapids, crackling leaves in haste to get from here to
there for no purpose other than to do it.

> cloudless sky
> enjoying the dog
> enjoying the river

Settling down for the evening on a mossy spot along the bank I am calmed by the river's steady flow. The water which I had passed over making my way here during the day now passes me by, bearing with it traces of the many soils and landscapes it drains: Blue Ridge escarpment, Shenandoah Valley effluvium, Piedmont loess, mingle in these waters, are the mud and shine of its passing. Also flowing, the shine of the bright moon, the dim halo of stars about it, and, in the dark woods, my own shining being—

> camping alone
> the crackle of small sticks
> in the fire
>
> —Jim Kacian

Notice how Jim Kacian has used human sound in contrast to nature's quiet, among other aspects, to help develop a definition of humanity in the context of natural "presence." But the "order" of this haibun's title is that everything of the natural world, including humanity, changes. Left unsaid, but hinted at, is that something like spirit, what the Chinese call Tao, does not change.

The following nature sketch is pure description without the figurative language of "Winter Haibun" or the extensive philosophizing of "The Order of Stars." Yet through a reliance on sense imagery it creates a subtly moving scene in which nature settles down for the night:

NIGHT VISITOR

Mockingbird song mingles with last random raindrops. Fading thunder carries off swift clouds: last glimmer of light drips from iris petals—deepening blue sky. Landing egret: stark white wings whisper close—it settles in sparkling reeds, clawed feet clutch wet grass. In dim glow black garden stones glisten between unfurling ferns: heavenly bamboo holds falling shadow amid delicate leaves. Nightfall quiets the mockingbird's cascading song.

> darkening foliage
> the egret
> now ghost-grey

> —Dennis Kalkbrenner

Notice how the use of short phrases and incomplete sentences reflects the intensity of the author's emotions as he observes this scene. And almost all of these phrases and sentences are images that could easily be subjects of a true "nature sketch," a quick suggestive painting or drawing of what we have seen in nature.

Haibun Narratives

Haibun narratives are little stories about how something in daily life has moved us to an experience of deep feeling. It could be a loved one, an ordinary chore, or a simple object. Sometimes for obvious reasons and sometimes for mysterious reasons these people, experiences, or things change our lives. Notice how a common houseplant that was left behind in an office becomes an emotional focus for the author:

AMARYLLIS

There was an amaryllis on the windowsill of my new office when I moved in. When I inherited the title and the office space, the plant, left behind in a career move, came along as well.

I'm not much of a houseplant-person, but I feel a basic responsibility and coerced affection for this ugly amaryllis, much as I would for a runt of a kitten left on my doorstep, even though I'm not a cat person.

The amaryllis has never bloomed. Green and supple, its four long, slender leaves sprawl outward to either side, out of proportion to the white plastic pot. The plant appears to be in a state of suspended animation: it doesn't grow, but it doesn't die. The sun touches it only through glass; the only breeze comes from the air-conditioning vent. I know how it feels.

> pot-bound
> the amaryllis
> on the water-stained sill

> —Cathy Drinkwater Better

The last line of the haibun's prose is full of emotion. The author seems to be talking as much about her life in her office as she is about the plant with which she has identified. And this emotion allows us to see the inner life of the plant so plainly described in the haiku.

The death of, or separation from, a loved one can be one of the most painful experiences in someone's life. Notice how understated the tone of this haibun is in comparison to the overwhelming nature of what has happened. See how all the emotion the author must feel is contained in this little narrative about coffee mugs:

PANTRY SHELF

Pottery shops were a weakness of yours. When we came upon one your eyes would lock on it. You'd glance at me with the words, sometimes unspoken: "Do we have time?—Yes, let's have a look." Usually, not looking for anything in particular—just the delight in seeing, touching and holding useful things crafted with care. When you just had to buy, we went for coffee mugs—you can never have too many! And so we had a shelf of them in our pantry—most were "yours" and a few were "mine."

six weeks after—
her coffee mugs
at the back of the shelf

—Cyril Childs

From time to time we are shocked or delighted by some surprise that occurs in something in our ordinary routine, what we do day in and day out, like brushing our teeth or getting dressed. Who could have imagined a surprise in these events or others like them, like doing the laundry?

LAUNDRY DAY

I never knew quilts had names until my mother mailed me pictures of the ones she had made, along with a note asking me to select my favorite as a gift. I chose one called Picket Fence.

I always wait for warm, breezy days to launder my quilt so it will dry as fluffy as it was when I first received it. I carefully place each clothespin along its border of tiny blue flowers that frame alternating shades of blue and white zigzagging across its whole, creating the delightful picket effect. When the quilt's dry I gather it into my arms as I remove the wooden pins and carry it to the house, holding it lightly to my chest so as not to crush the fluffiness. Once inside, I head straight for the bedroom and allow it to float in gentle folds upon the bed . . .

laundry day—
over the picket fence quilt
a tan and black snake

—Linda Jeannette Ward

Notice how the discussion of the quilt's pattern prepares us for the pattern of the snake's colors. And notice how the emphasis on the quilt's softness contrasts with the shocking presence of the snake.

Travel Haibun

Most of us travel for fun and adventure. We want to see beautiful and exciting things. Many of us want to connect with the wonder of wild nature. Others travel to learn something about some specific place. Still others are really on an introspective journey.

I wrote the following travel haibun to record a kind of adventure I had when I tried to locate the exact scene in the well-known painting "Kindred Spirits," which I reproduced on the cover of my haibun anthology *Journey to the Interior*. That painting embodied exactly what I felt our experience of nature should be.

KINDRED SPIRITS

I was hiking in the Catskill Mountains in late autumn. I had a special interest in the area: to locate the exact spot that was the scene of Asher Durand's well-known painting "Kindred Spirits." In the painting, Thomas Cole, the founder of the nineteenth-century Hudson River school of landscape painting, to which Durand belonged, and William Cullen Bryant, the nature poet who authored the renowned "Thanatopsis," stand next to each other on a ledge. They are surrounded by wilderness and overlooking an impressive river gorge—the two figures dwarfed by the natural scene.

None of the librarians in the Woodstock library, an old wooden building resembling a many-roomed one-room school house, could identify the painting or the area. With a little looking, however, I found several reproductions of the painting, one of which I Xeroxed, and references to the town of Palenville and to Kaaterskill Clove, the site of the painting. The next morning I set off for Palenville, a tiny community in the foothills of the Catskills. The attendant at one of the two Palenville gas stations hadn't heard of Kaaterskill Clove and couldn't help me. Nor could anyone help me in the local tavern. The last building in town was a combination gas station and diner. The clerk couldn't help me but said that the gentleman at a nearby table might. He was very old and wore worn-out clothes. I was hesitant to interrupt him but when I showed him the Xerox he immediately exclaimed, "That's Fawn's Leap!" I followed his directions, similar to the footpath described in one of the library art books, up the hill out of town to a turnout. There was litter all over the place and it didn't look promising, with dense overgrowth on the other side of the guardrail. I got out anyway and walked around. I looked up to see a rusted-out sign that said Kaaterskill Clove.

I found the ledge that Durand had placed Cole and Bryant on. It was smaller somehow and overgrown with saplings. The gorge was much less impressive than in the painting. Nor could I see the low falls depicted there. But I confirmed that this was the spot by locating the place where Durand would have had to stand to get the perspective in the painting. The place was absolutely still, except for the chickadees playing in the one pine tree at the overlook's edge and a lone pale brown leaf falling to the overlook, and I was mesmerized to be at that spot looking into that scene:

> Kaaterskill Clove:
> a pebbly patch of stream
> green with moss

Notice how the title of this haibun is not merely the title of the painting but is meant to incorporate the author's appreciation of the scene on which the painting was based. Notice, too, how the delicacy of the haiku, written over a century later, reflects the kind of appreciation celebrated in the painting.

Diary Haibun

A diary is a daily personal record of events, experiences, and observations. In diary haibun the things we record are more poetically expressed and perhaps more charged with emotion than an ordinary diary, for here we are consciously tending to a poetic record of our inner self, whether we travel across a country or stay right at home.

The following are the concluding sections of a chapbook-length diary of the author's hitchhiking trip across Canada. Note the direct, almost telegraphic, simple style in which the deep emotional impact of nature and the experience of travel are presented.

XIX.

Hour beyond hour in the darkness, adrift through sleep, I hear rain, rain awash more loudly than the waves of high tide. Wake to more rain, gradually, in gray light.

At first let-up, the other campers pack tents and gone. Solitude through tenacity. Eat in my tent, read. Near noon a yellow sun spreads moist wind over the sea. Gulls walk the sand with gathered wings. I go out to them. They run, look back, then fly out to a rock island near shore.

> waves break over rock—
> gulls, spray
> fly

Steam rises from beach logs in green light. Grass stalks hung with drops twist in the breeze.

Evening after all-day rain, sky clear, nighthawks slash above the trees. After such rain a long time to get fire started. I blow on it . . . coals burst orange and . . . turn from smoke in eyes. Coals dim. I blow hard and . . . dizzy. Sit as fire fades again. Blow once more, and damp wood finally catches. Galaxy of embers glow.

Finished eating, sip tea, write. Sharpen my pencil with a knife. Yellow shavings on pine needles shine in the glow of the fire. As I scribble, pages dampen with dew.

I walk to the beach to scrub pots, swirl the sand around, scrape down to a metal sheen. Look up across the water, to where summer constellations, Lyra and Aquila and Cygnus, shine beyond the mist. Constant calm rhythm of the surf stretches around. Stars thrash in the beach sand, glitter, and return to dark. Above the sea, Antares, the red heart of Scorpio, lingers in the eye.

> stars through twilit haze—
> even after the sky has cleared
> rain drips from the trees

XX.

After waking, I drag sleeping bag to beach, spread wet clothes in the sun, on dry sand. Walk beach all day, sit and read, do nothing.

> dense mist—
> in dawn light a gull
> again finds land

XXI.

Once more a morning, sky clear. Thin haze slides off the sea into the trees. Small cumulus scatter over the inland mountains. I break camp and head for the road. Hitch cross-island all day. "Ever seen such windy roads as on this island?" "Sure, back in Pennsylvania, even windier." "Naw."

Victoria, buy a few peaches, toss pits into the sea. To what avail time, waiting for the ferry.

> cross the straits
> through evening blue
> venus behind thin clouds

I lean on the rail. Tonight too, crossing Victoria ferry, white seagulls high in the air float with motionless wings. To what avail space.

In the distance the lights of Port Angeles begin to come on. A few bright stars above them.

[6/27–7/18/77]
—Tom Lynch

Tom Lynch's haibun, as evidenced by these sections, is very much like Bashō's *Narrow Path to the Interior* in its direct style, in which both natural and human experience are treated in moods varying from humorous to awesome.

The following is one of several diary haibun written on the death of the author's close friend. Notice how dense the imagery is and how the level of language and the manner of phrasing thoughts are beyond ordinary expression.

HAIBUN FOR DENNIS: DECEMBER 12, 1994

I needed to get out of the house. The obscenity of objects bare of him. At Blue Hill, the cliffs near the main path were covered with a thin sheet of ice where bluish lichen and patches of soaked moss showed through. Suddenly I noticed the intermittent water droplets between ice and rock, corpuscle-like black shapes. It was like looking at the movement of blood under a microscope. Somehow the horizontal pull of the pattern kept the submerged waterfall in unearthly suspension as all across the broad rock face the globes of water came curvetting down the six or seven inches before catching in the comb of ice, flexing between surfaces, and falling . . . Back at the front door it was as if I looked again through a window of ice.

> in the empty house
> prism light from the window
> soaks the woodwork
>
> —Judson Evans

Note how the images of ice, corpuscles, and trapped water express the anxious feeling of loss and how the light in the haiku offers an intangible sense of comfort.

CONCLUSION

To conclude, I would advise a number of things in your own practice of haibun. Get in the habit of keeping a journal or a diary of your daily events or travels. If something moves you, whether it is a person, place, or thing, it may be a good subject for a haibun. Develop a sensitivity to how haiku relate to the prose narratives of your haibun. Don't just tell a story; let your figurative language, word choice, and phrasing help carry the emotion in your narrative. Try exercises in nature haibun, narrative haibun, travel haibun, and diary haibun. Try a serious, high tone and style like Jim Kacian. Try a more casual, light tone and style like Tom Lynch or Sally Secor. And try a simple nature sketch like Dennis Kalkbrenner. Even try your hand at fiction or a more experimental prose style. And remember, the prose in your haibun lets your emotions loose, the haiku focus your feeling.

Expressing Your Feeling: Tanka

TANKA IS ONE OF THE OLDEST and, up to the modern period, the most widely written form of Japanese poetry. Of all the haiku-related poetic forms, tanka is most like what we call lyric poetry—that is, poetry filled with highly personal and emotional expression. In it we say how we feel about those close to us, and what is going on with our thoughts and feelings, no matter what kinds of experiences we are having. But usually tanka, which was most often written in five lines or phrases in a 5-7-5-7-7 syllable pattern, connect these thoughts and emotions to nature. And, as in lyric poetry, figurative expression, such as comparisons like metaphor and simile, are allowed. In other words, with tanka you can let your imagination help you to express your feeling.

EXAMPLES OF TANKA

Here are two examples of contemporary American Tanka:

We walk this morning
barefoot through the dewy grass,
your steps next to mine.
At nine, after you had gone,
I could find no trace of us.

—Anita Wintz

a mountain road
at summer's end
I search
for the warmth of your embrace
before the autumn wind

—Yu Chang

Notice how both authors connect their feelings about their loved one to the patterns of nature. The first tanka compares the fleeting nature of love or time spent with a loved one to the morning dew that evaporates in the sunlight. The second one presents the author's feelings about being separated from his loved one, perhaps permanently, through the metaphor of the approaching season of autumn and the diminishing of natural beauty and liveliness. And the love theme depicted in both is by far the most common one in all tanka. Notice also that the first tanka sticks exactly to the 5-7-5-7-7 pattern, which was the case for all Japanese tanka until the modern period, while the second one considerably pares down that pattern and is typical of modern American tanka. Both of these examples sound like a traditional Japanese tanka in the expression of their emotion. That most Japanese tanka from its earliest appearance to the present retains the 5-7-5-7-7 syllable pattern is understandable since most Japanese poetry until the modern period was written in lines or phrases of five or seven syllables or, really, sound units.

CLASSICAL JAPANESE TANKA

From the earliest period, at least from the eighth century, Japanese tanka were collected in anthologies that were sponsored by and included members of the royal court. Tanka, which may be translated as "short song," addressed such themes as natural beauty, love, the impermanence of life, the activities of ordinary people, and separation from loved ones. Consider the following two examples of early court tanka:

I wait for you	so dimly
oh! with tender passion	over the Akashi Bay
as in my house	in pale blue light
the bamboo blinds stir	a boat passes behind the islands
blown by autumn wind	and I am touched by it
—Princess Nukada	—Kakinomoto no Hitomaro

Notice how these tanka express tender feelings connected with nature, as did most court tanka. Both examples are from the seventh century. The second one is in fact by the first important figure in Japanese poetry. Notice how both tanka name their emotion, the first as "tender passion" and the second as being "touched." If we remember the word *aware* (to be touched) when we look at these tanka, we can understand why the phrase *mono no aware* ("to be touched by things") was such an important idea in tanka writing, as it also was later with the development of haiku. Notice the delicate imagery of the stirring bamboo blinds in the first tanka and the stillness of a boat passing some islands in hazy light in the second. Both illustrate *mono no aware* and the central emotional tone of traditional Japanese tanka. And both illustrate two major themes of tanka: addressing a real or imagined beloved, in the first, and responding to the beauty of a natural scene, in the second.

Saigyō, a twelfth-century monk and wandering poet, was a transitional figure in Japanese tanka who had a great influence on Bashō. I have discussed Saigyō in my courses on Japanese literature as well as those on Zen Buddhism. Here are two examples that might make us recall the different moods of Bashō's haiku and haibun:

even a person   such loneliness!
who has disciplined his emotion   if there were just someone
is overcome with feeling: also in this situation:
a snipe rises from the marsh   our hermits' huts side by side
into the autumn twilight   in a mountain village for winter

As a monk, Saigyō was supposed to be unattached to worldly sensations, as he acknowledges in the first two lines of the first tanka. But Saigyō is one of Japan's great nature poets, and he often wrote about the effects of natural beauty upon his feelings and state of mind. Notice how the last two lines describe such beauty and are like a miniature haiku on autumn beauty, in which the loneliness of the setting is accentuated by the rising bird. The second tanka reminds us of Bashō's "Snowball" haibun in its mischievous tone. Saigyō spent much time wandering alone in nature. Yet he often, like Bashō, lived in a little hut near some village. Again, even if Saigyō wrote his best tanka celebrating his loneliness in nature and the peace that it brought to his mind, he was, like Bashō, fond of companionship and, as he is well aware, needed both equally.

MODERN JAPANESE TANKA

Modern Japanese tanka went through the same types of experimentation as other Japanese literary forms. The 5-7-5-7-7 pattern was sometimes loosened up. Some tanka were written in one horizontal line and some had less than five lines or phrases. Some continued to explore their authors' feelings in nature in a romantic way while others presented realistic "sketches from nature" or the many styles and approaches found in modern world poetry. One of the most important early modern tanka writers was Ishikawa Takuboku, who was writing at the end of the nineteenth century and the beginning of the twentieth century. Notice how in the following two tanka the natural world is left out and the mood of each is connected to the author's inner feelings about the ordinary events of his life:

I work	I shut my eyes
and work still my life	but nothing whatsoever
continues	surfaces in my mind
to be the same as ever	in my utter loneliness
I look at my hands	I open them up again

Notice the contrast between the stark mood of alienation and the ordinary phrasing with which these tanka are expressed. They are like overhearing someone's conversation or hearing their inner thoughts. But tanka like this allowed later tanka writers to consider expressing feelings that were quite unlike the court poetry.

In 1987 a young Japanese high school teacher, Tawara Machi, published a collection of tanka called *Salad Anniversary*. It became a best-selling work, and she became a television celebrity. Notice how, in the following examples, the author returns to the natural beauty of court poetry but transforms that style of sensitive feeling into an expression of more challenging and more modern inner feeling:

I wait for spring	cherry blossoms
with an empty heart	cherry blossoms cherry blossoms
in March	begin blooming
gazing at late blossoming plum	stop blooming and as it was before
with you	the same park

Something has changed in how poets look at nature and at their own life. Somehow the beauty of nature does not have the overpowering effect that it had in the tradition of court poetry. A very modern tone that even seems to include some kind of criticism of that kind of feeling is expressed here. The second tanka is in fact almost overly dramatic since cherry blossoms are the single most often used image of beauty in Japan. The author seems to do this by pointing out the ordinariness of these beautiful blossoms. They come and go, she tells us, and the park they blossom in is still the same old park.

MODERN AMERICAN TANKA

Take a look at a modern American tanka that might have been influenced by Takuboku. But notice the humorous way in which the author has made over such tanka through a more modern-sounding tone of emotion, one that is directed to our everyday life:

> this being human
> each new day choices,
> chores and emotions—
> hands in the sinkwater and
> the children call for more
>
> —Tom Clausen

This poem, which was the judge's tanka for the 1999 Tanka Splendor Awards anthology, takes the often challenging experiences of family life as it is related in a higher-toned philosophic way in the tanka's first three lines and illustrates this condition with a concrete example that is amusing in itself and expressed in a conversational way. This seems to imply that the author doesn't take the first three lines seriously and is a bit amused by the possibly frustrating situation in which, probably exhausted, he is finished with dinner but his children aren't.

The natural world is left out of Tom Clausen's tanka, which, in its way, is centered on the ups and downs we all face as human beings. But by far most American tanka, beginning with the first compositions in the 1970s, is about either nature or love. Here are two examples that exhibit these themes. Notice the distinct difference in the presented mood:

watching
the pear tree blossom
a new sorrow—
this year it is my turn
to leave

    —Cherie Hunter Day

it was spring
but wind-driven rain
was so bad
and so good
we joined umbrellas

    —Watha Lambert

There is an undefined melancholy in the first tanka. Despite the beauty of the pear blossoms the author is saddened. The pear tree is beginning to blossom again as it always has. But this time the author has to experience some unnamed separation made more painful by the beauty of the pear tree she has always enjoyed. In the second, the for-the-moment bother of heavy spring rain becomes a celebration of new things: both the season, when new flowers bloom, and the possibility of the beginning of a new or renewed friendship symbolized by the touching umbrellas. Though expressed in the tanka form and on the traditional tanka themes of nature and human affection, each of these sound very much like modern American poetry in general.

This is both good and bad. American tanka, like American haibun, is still experimenting with its form. Unlike American haiku and senryu, which have a recognized style and acknowledged masters, tanka is still finding its appropriate style and values. This may be because it is so much like modern poetry in its aims and modes of expression, and because modern American poetry has been able to provide a very fruitful outlet. Nonetheless, there is a delicacy of linking emotion to nature and a concentrated boldness in expressing one's deepest emotion in tanka that is not quite like anything else in modern poetry. There are already a number of strong voices in tanka and several important collections. There are also a few American tanka journals and a major annual tanka competition. In other words, tanka is very much in an exploratory stage.

SUBJECTS IN AMERICAN TANKA

Nature

There are three main subjects in American tanka: nature, love, and one's psychological situation. All of these may be appreciated in the context of my discussion of the development of Japanese tanka. But there is a decidedly American way of expressing personal experience that makes American tanka sometimes unique. Poetry, specifically tanka, connects human emotion with nature because nature seems to coax from us emotions similar to what we have for other people. It is also a kind of immense emotional backdrop within which we can place our own private emotional drama. And it provides stimulating occasions of beauty that we can celebrate. Notice the relationship between nature and the author's feeling for his pet dog in the following:

> morning walk
> earlier than usual
> squirrels not out yet
> > our dog tugs at my heart
> > instead of a leash
>
> —David Rice

The first three lines tell us that the author is well-acquainted with the regular patterns of nature and that he enjoys them. We sense that he appreciates the presence of the squirrels and that they delight him. But the squirrels are not out yet, so his feelings are directed to his companion dog. Perhaps the absence of the squirrels intensifies his feeling for his dog, which may itself be seen now as not so far distant in nature from the squirrels. And this insight fills the author with deep feeling. The following two tanka both examine the state of being up late at night and hearing the sounds of nature:

drone of cricket song . . .
the ebb -
and - flow
of my thoughts
this sleepless night

—Kenneth Tanemura

it was
the night bird
that woke me
but it is the sound of nothing
that keeps me awake

—Lequita Vance

The wonderful first tanka uses the cricket song as a pure metaphor for the author's wandering thoughts on a sleepless night. The phrasing and punctuation reinforce the mood of this poem on the perfect union of human awareness and natural liveliness. That is, the author is far from complaining about the late-night cricket sound. In the second tanka there is an obvious complaint: the bird woke the author up. But this simple occurrence leads her to a profound experience of stillness. Many of us have woken up in the middle of the night and found ourselves disoriented by the silence and lack of any activity. It is as if we were seeing our room and, for that matter, the world for the first time. Sometimes we are disturbed by the quiet. Sometimes we are in awe of it. Something of both seems to be suggested in this tanka's last two lines. But there is also a bit of humor implied if we stretch our imagination. The night bird can be seen as a little Zen master who brings his disciple to an experience of enlightenment by making a sharp sound. Zen masters also used *koans*, mental puzzles, to help a student find enlightenment. Students would ponder the koan until they thought they had solved its meaning. One famous koan is: What is the sound of one hand clapping? Of course there is no rational answer. And that is the point. Many koans used nature as a metaphor for states of mind. To extend the joke, the author may be seen as staying awake to solve a koan about the meaning of nothingness posed to her by the little bird master.

This deeper kind of understanding aroused in us by nature is found in the following tanka:

> weeding in the garden
> humming to myself
> suddenly a mourning dove
> calls from me some sadness
> I can't quite name

> —Mary Lou Bittle-DeLapa

We recognize the experience of the joyful communion with nature that gardening brings to many people. Those of us who have heard a mourning dove know that its call is mournful; it is this haunting sound that gave the bird its name. But in this tanka the author seems to be moved to a higher feeling of sadness, one we associate with nature haiku and the idea of sabi. What exactly that sadness is the author doesn't know. Perhaps it is a profound understanding about how things live and die, like the plants and weeds in her garden. But we have seen earlier tanka writers just as powerfully moved by some undefined feeling provoked by nature. And this kind of feeling makes a truly great tanka.

Love

Love is the most common subject of American tanka. The intense affection we feel for a life companion, a member of our family, or a close friend can be experienced in many different kinds of moods, which tanka helps us to express. These moods may be categorized more or less in terms of negative feeling, positive feeling, or an ambiguous combination of negative and positive feeling. The negative feelings about love include the unwished-for end of a relationship with someone we cared deeply about. Notice the ambiguity of the situation in the following example:

> box after box
> hauled up the stairs
> no time
> to think how
> I shall leave you
>
> —Connie Meester

Has the author lost her companion to death? Are they merely separating after having shared life in the same house? Consider the metaphor of the boxes, which, though they contain objects that remind the author of her companion, come to represent the author's attempt to resolve the deep disruption in her emotional life. If only she could, she would place that disruption in a box and store it somewhere. But her humanity doesn't allow this and so she expresses herself through this very tanka.

Have you ever cared for someone so much that your whole life felt more alive and you could hardly contain your joy? Look as this tanka, which captures the feelings that are a part of being in love:

> in the crystal vase
> arranging all the flowers
> it can hold
> no more room in me
> so filled am I with you
>
> —Robert Henry Poulin

This tanka is built on a simple metaphor comparing a vase totally filled with flowers to the author being totally filled with love for his companion. He separates the poem into the vase half of the metaphor in the first three lines and his own emotion in the last two lines, a common structural device that helps distinguish human emotion from the natural imagery that illustrates it. But look how deftly the author has chosen his words and how he breaks the two parts of the metaphor.

Family life offers endless experiences of the deepest affection human beings can know. Look at this moving example from *A Work of Love*, the small tanka collection by Tom Clausen about the trials, tribulations, and emotional rewards of bringing up children:

> I look over
> the three sleeping bodies
> beside me—
> to think a whole decade
> I felt all alone

Perhaps the family is on a camping trip. Perhaps the young children want to be comforted by their parents in bed. All the positive emotion the author feels for his family is suddenly contained in their sleeping bodies. Perhaps looking at the innocence he sees there allows him to realize how truly lonely he was before he had a family.

Sometimes the thought of the absence or possible loss of a loved one can produce conflicting emotions. Compare the following two tanka:

> when I think
> that we may never
> meet again . . .
> this hillside of aspens
> endlessly fluttering
>
> —Larry Kimmel

> this waiting
> in the empty room
> for her call
> dry November leaves
> litter the ground
>
> —Bruce Ross

Both tanka structure their nature metaphors with a break after the third line just like Robert Henry Poulin's crystal vase tanka did. The first tanka's metaphor is a little complex. If you have ever seen quaking aspen trees blown by the wind, you might appreciate the depth of this metaphor. The individual leaves hang down from a long stem and literally quake. The tree seems very agitated, which is a perfect metaphor for the state the author would be in if he never again saw the person for whom he has affection. The second tanka is more moody. I am not really in an empty room, but it is emotionally empty because my companion is not there. The nature metaphor is obvious in its imagery of the desolation associated with autumn that provides a straightforward example of my downhearted state.

Psychological States

A final common theme in American tanka is the presentation of an author's psychological response to the varied situations of life. Consider the following:

> cold November day
> the squirrel's comings and goings
> no longer hidden
> my doctor's
> short list of options
>
> —Francine Porad

The author is suffering the kind of serious illness that is so complicated that a number of solutions must be carefully considered. She sees a squirrel in late autumn, possibly collecting leaves for its nest or burying acorns in preparation for winter. These activities become an actual metaphor for her thoughts about her illness. The squirrel, of necessity, must make its preparations just as she, now that her options are out in the open like the squirrel, must also make her decisions about her illness.

Sometimes we feel lonely even if we are surrounded by people. Here is an example of that state from *No Love Poems*, a fine collection of tanka by Kenneth Tanemura about the difficulties of being a teenager:

> alone in a crowd:
> even the seat
> in this cafe
> doesn't
> fit

Notice how the gradual shortening of the line lengths in this tanka reflect the author's discomfort—he is so self-conscious that he feels uncomfortable sitting on an ordinary seat. He feels ground down by his loneliness and ground into his seat by that emotion.

Now look at the following tanka, which, in contrasting moods, express a positive communion with the living pattern of nature:

On the morning bus
    I look past the handsome face
to the red maple.
    When did it happen—the change
in the leaves, the change in me?

—Doris Heitmeyer

We feed the ducks
you and I
and
the laughing little boy you
have begun to become.

—Pamela Miller Ness

Both tanka are about emotional breakthroughs. In the first, the author, on an ordinary day, while riding a bus, powerfully senses something in the bright red autumn maple leaves that goes beyond the normally desired physical beauty of a stranger's appearance. In other words, the red leaves, which become a metaphor of the higher beauty in nature and its patterns, provide as deep a satisfaction as that found in the affection we have for other people. Notice how the punctuation in the last two lines and the overall phrasing reinforce the philosophic tone of this introspective tanka. What the exact nature of the author's breakthrough is we don't know, but this indefiniteness adds to the depth of the tanka. The second tanka, in contrast, celebrates the liveliness and joy found in nature and connects these qualities to the author's companion, who seems coaxed into childlike delight by the experience described in the tanka. Notice how this new childlike state becomes personified as a third person. Notice how the simple phrasing and short line lengths reflect this childlike state and the author's appreciation of it. There is a light and bubbly tone here that also reflects the tanka's subject.

There are other situations that can be compared to the kind of subtle feeling that the priest Saigyō felt in his isolation in nature. Consider these tanka by Anna Holley:

If the moon	a long shadow
has no other place	follows behind me
to lodge tonight,	on the road;
I'll offer my heart	never will I be able
empty of all light	to outrun the past

Both tanka take their emotional color from a very deep level of introspection. The last line of the first is too serious for us to take it for a playful metaphor on the moon as a traveler without lodging for the night. The author's heart is without light not because she doesn't have a companion to share her affections with, but because she has emptied herself of all ordinary feeling. She is searching for some deeper feeling and finds it, much as Saigyō did, in many tanka on the moon, in the moodiness and metaphysical emptiness of the moonlight. The second tanka also uses a personification to support its serious subject. The author's shadow is like a person running after her. To see it simply as her past would make this tanka too superficial and almost clichéd. But it is not really the past she is talking about. Rather, she is offering an insight into the very basic nature of what it means to be simply alive. If we are deeply honest and, like Saigyō in his isolation, filter out the often mindless external stimulation that fills up our daily lives, we might arrive at the stark emotional state of this tanka. We can appreciate it for this moodiness. But we can also realize that such moodiness often comes just before an extraordinarily deep insight, as this tanka perhaps has already implied in its philosophically expressed thought.

CONCLUSION

To sum up, I would offer some advice to those who would like to write tanka. Modern tanka is a loose form, but stick to the five-line pattern. Try your hand at a perfect 5-7-5-7-7 syllable pattern. And remember, more and more American tanka is written in short-long-short-long-long, as well as many other patterns. Try writing tanka in shorter line lengths as well as more complex, longer line lengths and try to correlate the emotional mood of your tanka, whether joyful or serious, with these line lengths. Try to write with modern-sounding words and phrasing. And while it is not always necessary, as you can see by the examples presented here, in your tanka, try to connect your emotions to nature. Use figurative language where you need to, but don't overdo it. In other words, don't write bad poetry with clichéd feeling, weak figurative expression, and an unoriginal manner of phrasing. Try to sound fresh and contemporary, but don't avoid the more serious, higher tone. Try your hand at expressing silly, everyday experiences through tanka, but also try to capture those undefined elevated feelings provoked by nature. Try to write an outright comparison between your feelings and imagery taken from nature, separating the two parts after the third line. Try to write a more subtle metaphor that incorporates the whole tanka. And, if you can, try to evoke the compassion we can feel when we are moved by something in nature or by our affections for another human being.

Drawing a Picture: Haiga

A HAIGA IS NOT SO MUCH an illustration of a haiku as an artistic expression of the spirit of the haiku's feeling. In other words, it is a drawing that complements and responds to the haiku.

AMERICAN HAIGA

Let us look again at my spring turtles haiku. My brother had been with me when I spotted them. I pointed them out to him, and we both watched them for some time. I sent him my haiku on the turtles, and he came up with a drawing to accompany my haiku. Now look at his rendering with my haiku inserted into it:

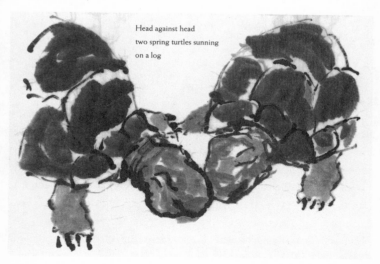

Head against head
two spring turtles sunning
on a log

You will notice several characteristics of American haiga in this work. First of all, the drawing captures the spirit of the haiku, which is about the humanlike nature of the turtles' heads leaning on each other. The drawing focuses on those heads and includes only a part of the rest of the turtles' bodies. A second feature is that the turtles are not drawn with realistic precision as if this were a photographic illustration for a biology textbook. You feel the turtles' contentment lying in the sun after a long winter. Their eyes are closed, and there is even the hint of a little smile on their faces. The segments of their shells are suggested rather than realistically drawn. Moreover, the black watercolor's gray washed-out tones, in contrast with the darker lines that outline some of the more obvious structure of the turtles' bodies, add to the suggestive, almost abstract quality of the drawing. Overall, this haiga—and all haiga—have the characteristic of being a sketch rather than a polished drawing or painting. This is in keeping with the Zen Buddhist philosophy of art that influenced both haiku and haiga. In this philosophy, the artist is supposed to respond quickly to what he or she sees or experiences. This suits haiku perfectly because haiku is supposed to be an insightful presentation of what is happening in a given moment of time. This aesthetic would therefore suit even more the haiga method of a quick sketch of what is seen or experienced. Furthermore, my brother's ink drawing not only captures the spirit of my haiku but enlivens it.

CLASSICAL JAPANESE HAIGA

There is a tradition in China that allows someone to practice many art forms. For example, the well-known eighth-century Chinese poet and painter Wang Wei is said to be the father of monochrome—art done in different shades of the same color—landscape painting. The monochrome style is like the traditional Japanese *sumi-e*, or black ink, painting illustrated by the spring turtles drawing. Like Wang Wei, Yosa Buson, an eighteenth-century poet considered one of the four great masters of Japanese haiku, was also a widely respected painter. Here is a section from Bashō's travel haibun *Narrow Path to the Interior* and the haiga that Buson did to accompany it:

On the outskirts of this post town was a huge chestnut tree. A priest was living in seclusion in its shade. I was reminded of the deep mountains where the poet Saigyō had picked chestnuts. I took out a piece of paper and wrote the following:

The Chinese character for "chestnut" means "western tree," the direction of the Buddhist Paradise. Priest Gyōki used chestnut wood for his walking stick and as a support of his house.

people of this world
do not notice its wonderful blossoms—
the chestnut by the cave

Bashō's haiku depicts the beauty of the wild chestnut, which has sprigs of brilliant white blossoms with tiny purple veins. People who don't venture into the wilderness, of course, could not view this beauty. But such a simple understanding of the haiku wouldn't do justice to Bashō. He is seeing in the beauty of the wild tree a symbol of the spiritual wisdom of priests like Saigyō, who lived in such wilderness in order to cultivate their inner lives. Buson's haiga captures this symbolism. In a small, modest hut a priest is sitting in a doorway, perhaps meditating. The blossoming chestnut tree, the symbol of his wisdom, stands next to the hut and almost covers half of it. We have here the impression of a selfless, humble person for whom beauty and wisdom take priority over everything else. Unlike Bashō, who only created simple haiga drawings like this treatment of the chestnut tree, Buson went on to include more formal painting as an acceptable approach to haiga so that today in Japan both simple ink sketches and bright-colored paintings and drawings are considered haiga.

Most Chinese and Japanese art takes nature as its subject. Within the long tradition of this art there are two principal themes: flowers and landscapes. In fact, when students learn to draw in the sumi-e style, they first practice drawing four kinds of flowers. For many years I have lived with the following haiga by Bashō on my wall. I can no longer remember where I found it. Nor was I able to read the old script in which Bashō wrote his haiku. But a Japanese professor I know made a literal translation into modern Japanese for me. I did the rest and translated Bashō's haiku:

> mountain path . . .
> I am moved by something touching
> about these violets

Once again we have a poet wandering in wild nature. The simple wild violets in the grass beside the path are not as dramatic as the chestnut tree. In fact, violets are so tiny they might be overlooked. But there was something about them that caught Bashō's attention. Perhaps it was their modest simplicity and understated beauty with their purplish-blue petals. And further, these characteristics might suggest to Bashō the brief span of the flowers' lives and beauty. Bashō also might have been struck to find such simple beauty that, except for

his chance attention, would have gone unnoticed. The flowers then could come to represent some immaterial truth. They could even make one meditate upon how fast our lives go by.

In Bashō's haiga to

the left, notice how the violets are placed in a small space in the lower right-hand corner to emphasize their simplicity. Notice all the white space, which might represent the indefinite nature of their beauty. The haiku is written in the upper left-hand corner in long, flowing, vertical script, as if it were the standing Bashō looking down on these modest flowers. This haiga, as a whole, despite the realistic treatment of the violets themselves, has, like the spring turtles, a very abstract feel to it.

CLASSICAL SUBJECTS OF HAIGA

Bamboo

Bamboo is one of the most common subjects in Chinese and Japanese art. In China it came to symbolize the superior person, who could adapt to the times without losing sight of his or her essential nature. One can see this symbolism in the long, slender trunks of bamboo that bend in the wind without breaking. The leaves themselves offered a special interest in the suggestiveness of their movement when agitated by a hint of breeze. In fact, the leaves rather than the trunk were the more common artistic focus. To the right is an example of modern American haiga by Kay F. Anderson that is very much in tune with this classical subject.

Notice the artist's abbreviated treatment of the two trunks and how the one leaf stem with its two leaves hangs out in empty space. The shading on these trunks

just as it is
moonlight
on the old bamboo

Kay '97

is an effect of the moonlight. The haiku is set modestly in the lower right corner to exemplify the simplicity expressed in it. In fact, it is almost as if a monk were sitting beneath the bamboo and contemplating its beauty. "Just as it is" is a Zen Buddhist phrase that refers to seeing everything without preconception or mental or emotional prejudice. So the poet has come upon still bamboo in moonlight. Something about this touches her. In a sense, the moonlight is making her feel the inner nature of this old bamboo. The leaves dangling out into the moonlight hint at some higher nature to this feeling, as if they were reaching toward the source of this feeling.

Landscape

The other principal theme of oriental nature painting is the landscape. In these paintings human figures were tiny specs in an immense landscape. This immensity was considered an object of and setting for contemplation. The many folds and indentations of a mountain were especially celebrated. Contour and shading became a representation of the changeable quality of nature, which in turn came to reflect our own lives. Yet the suggestiveness of these often remote places conjured up some of the deepest feeling available to us. Here is another example of a modern haiga in the classical fashion. To the left, Susan Frame's painting "Jutting Rock" complements Francine Porad's haiku.

Notice how the activity of the mountain rock's contours and the flowing

jutting rock
the waterfall's two paths
to a quiet pool

iwa osi te
taki futasuji ni
oti ni keri

of the waterfall seem, despite such movement, to create a placid scene. The Chinese calligraphy of the haiku at the bottom of the falls steadies the haiga and comes to reflect the haiku's quiet pool. This haiga captures the blending of movement and stillness so valued in haiku and haiga.

MODERN AMERICAN HAIGA

Still, modern American haiga has come to be expressed in many types of materials, styles, and approaches unlike anything in classical haiga. American haiga "modernizes" traditional Japanese subject matter, technique, and medium, shying away from the delicately abstract sumi-e treatment of classical haiga as much as it relies on it. Some of the more innovative directions are related to the Western traditions of visual poetry, in which the words of a poem make an actual concrete picture of what the poem is about; collage, in which different kinds of things are thrown together in a piece of art but which all relate in some way to the work's central mood; and expressionist art, in which the external representation of things is distorted in order to express an inner mood or emotion. But in overall practice, modern American haiga seems easily related to classical haiga.

HAIGA BY CHILDREN

Drawing comes naturally to children. At the haiku table during the spring 1999 Japan-America Society of Vermont's Japanese festival I set up a work space with felt-tipped colored pens and drawing paper. When someone composed a haiku I suggested that they also create a drawing to go with it. One of these visitors was the teenaged boy who wrote the haiku:

> nothing happening
> just another day
> nothing happening

After some thought he began to draw. What he came up with was a stark brown, empty couch in the middle of the sheet of paper. Nothing else. He had drawn something to perfectly complement the mood of his haiku. Nothing is happening. Even the couch he would normally spend so much time on is empty.

Another visitor was the young girl who wrote this senryu about taiko drumming:

> Japanese festival
> I put my fingers in my ears
> for the taiko drumming

After some coaxing she drew a drum with two sticks floating in the air above it and near it a portrait of her head and arms with her fingers in her ears, all in all an amusing representation of her experience. Even more to the point was the haiga of a third visitor, an even younger girl. She came up to the table with her mother and sat down. As she sat down she dropped something under the table, which turned out to be a paper star. In fact, she had just made it at a Japanese origami, or paper folding, workshop. After we discussed what happened she drew a picture of the paper star in the middle of her paper to go with this haiku, which she wrote below it:

> I lost
> my origami star under the table
> I found it!

Not bad for a first try.

COLLABORATION IN HAIGA

The collaboration of a haiku poet and an artist is a traditional aspect of the haiga. When I organized my first collection of haiku in the late 1980s I asked my friend A. Aiko Horiuchi to choose one haiku from each of the collection's four parts. One she chose is this haiku:

> the lumpy birds squat
> on dripping telephone wire.
> heavy winter rain

I like the moodiness of this haiku, but mostly I like the fact that the birds are lumpy. It somehow makes them and their experience more personal. You could almost identify with these birds. Here is what A. Aiko Horiuchi came up with:

The composition and balance in this painting is really accomplished. But there is also a kind of humor here. The birds are situated on a wire that is at an angle. And they are really quite lumpy. They are waiting out the heavy rain, but one can almost imagine a kind of teeter-totter effect here where unaccountably the one bird is holding up the other two birds. The birds' perky faces add to the suggestion of mischief.

MODERN APPROACHES TO HAIGA

Humor

There are a number of approaches that modern American haiga takes in relation to its subjects. One of these is humor. One haiku by Bashō on a frog is the most recognized haiku in the world. It is said to mark a change in the way Bashō thought about haiku. Rather than make comic jokes through haiku like many of the haiku poets of his day, he attempted to connect with the lively aspects of the natural world to reveal their inner natures. Some even thought this frog haiku represented a Zen Buddhist spiritual breakthrough in which the sound of the splash in the haiku made Bashō suddenly see how perfectly in the moment all things really were. But others saw the haiku as simply ordinary or even a joke to parody. Here is Bashō's haiku and a parody of it by one of his contemporaries:

the old pond—
a frog jumps in:
the sound of water

the old pond—
if Bashō were here
I'd jump in myself

Here is a haiga that reflects Bashō's haiku in a humorous way. It is by Stephen Addiss, a well-known authority on haiga. Look for the humorous elements in it:

Old pond paved over
into a parking lot

one frog
still singing
AS

Stephen Addiss's haiga begins with Bashō's first line, so we know he is thinking about that haiku. But the haiga is really an ecological statement. Addiss is perhaps offering a direct response to the famous song about paving Paradise. Here is that parking lot, and, amazingly, here still is Bashō's frog. The parody in itself is amusing. But look at the goofy expression on the frog's face and notice how it is hanging on for dear life, a metaphor for the last bit of natural paradise.

Abstraction

Another major approach in modern American haiga is the technique of true abstraction. The first example below is again by Stephen Addiss; the second is by Karen Klein. Notice how the nonrepresentational drawing in each relates to the painted haiku. What do these forms suggest to you:

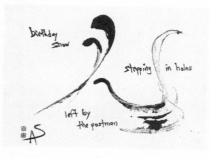

The charm of Stephen Addiss's haiku is evident. It is his birthday, and he is following the tracks of the person who may have delivered his birthday cards. If the drawing is of swirls of snow, it would make sense that the author would want to walk in an established path. As they say, nothing stops a postman from delivering the mail. We are all happy on our birthday, and the haiku and the gaily drawn swirls here reflect this mood. The author, through his haiga, is figuratively engulfed by this happiness. It is the end of winter in Karen Klein's haiga, and everything is bare, yet the little green shoots of parsley have sprouted under the cold frame—a protective covering for plants in cold weather. The bowlike abstract figure that surrounds the haiku suggests this cold frame. Further, the placing of the haiku's phrases is significant. The encircled bare trees are still in the grip of winter. The phrases "under the" and "cold frame" are situated to reinforce their meaning. And the "new parsley" is placed in the large opening space of the free ends as if to symbolize winter's bleakness opening up to spring.

Simplicity

A third major approach is through the motif of simplicity. You may have heard the expression "Less is more." In haiku and haiga this is even more so. In fact, the technique of suggestiveness is a central feature of all Chinese and, especially, Japanese art and literature. The tiny haiku form needs to be suggestive in order to summon up its deep feeling for the reader or listener. The drawing in haiga goes along with this sense of brevity. In fact, some Japanese Zen Buddhist

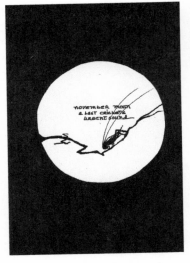

paintings are only one character, or "letter," long. That character has a recognizable meaning—for example, "silence." The artistry here comes from the elegance of the calligraphy and the starkness of the black ink against the stark white background. In such instances the artistry creates an abstract visualization of the meaning of the character. So a character, or "letter," can broaden out into absolute silence as a haiku can broaden out into the mood of a season. Both the above and following haiga, the first by Eugenie Waldteufel, and the second by Nasira Alma, consider the period at the end of autumn and the beginning of winter.

The end of autumn is made concrete in the figure of the little cricket. As winter approaches, the cricket can no longer stay outside unprotected. Its "urgent" call is meant to remind us that winter is coming with its coldness and snow. This point is more particularized because this cricket is the "last" to sing before winter. The artist has highlighted

first snow

new moon

silence

this dramatic event by placing the dark form of the cricket on a bare twig encircled by the bright full moon. Notice how pure darkness, perhaps a symbol of winter, surrounds the moon. This darkness consists of the same stark black color as the cricket and twig and suggests the stark absence of natural life that comes with winter. Notice the delicately drawn antennae that bend over the haiku to suggest the frailty of the cricket's situation. Nasira Alma's haiga is pure simplicity. Three housetops are sketched in a few simple lines. They are balanced by the three simple phrases of the haiku. The moon and snow are placed above the houses, as they should be. It is night. Everyone is sleeping. So the "silence" of the haiku is placed below the roofs where the people are inhabiting the evening stillness. Notice how the very brevity of the haiku and the drawing emphasize the silence.

Movement

A fourth major approach to American haiga represents some form of movement in order to give the haiga a visual aspect of activity. This dynamic quality can be presented in a more or less direct manner. Below is one of my haiga that presents a more subtle treatment of movement.

I had been visiting a beaver pond in the late fall, long after all the color had left the scene. It was absolutely still. There were no birds and no beaver. For that matter there were no other people either. There was

```
bent over
to its perfect reflection
autumn reed
```

no sound and no movement. Yet there was a suggestion of movement in the way a solitary brown reed was bent over to its reflection. That simple suggestion of movement seemed to dominate the otherwise still setting for me. Notice how the drawing of the reflection is in fact not quite perfect. And notice how the few blades of pond grass emphasize the suggestion of movement in their gentle curved forms.

Eye-ku

There is a kind of haiku derived from picture poetry that is called "eye-ku." In it the words that make up the haiku create a literal picture that relates to the meaning of the words. Look at this haiku:

migrating geese

one falls farther and farther

behind

—Charles Dickson

In this haiku, the slow goose is reflected by the single word *behind*, which is set very far behind and below the phrase "migrating geese," a representation of the flock it should be with. The very long second line marks the distance between that flock and the lone goose. The visual presentation here is very much like a haiga. Marlene Mountain takes this technique one step further by eliminating all the verbal description in her presentation of the frog's essence in its leap:

Beginning with the solitary "f" at the beginning of the third line, which is at "ground level," the remaining letters of "frog" are spread out in an arc in the second and first lines to be finally "reconstituted" to the far right in the third line as the complete word *frog* and the visual expression of its landing.

Stillness

A final major approach in modern American haiga is through the presentation of stillness. Bashō is said to have experienced another major breakthrough in his haiku writing in the following:

> on a dead branch
> the crow settles—
> autumn evening

It is commonly thought that Bashō introduced the moody state of sabi as a major feature of haiku with this poem. This haiku evokes a selfless union with the mood of sabi in nature, here represented through stark images of inevitable change—the dead branch, autumn, evening. A crow adds its dark presence to these images and "settles" into the scene. There is a sense of a somber spiritual awakening in this haiku that has revealed some basic truth about nature. Everything in this haiku is in a state of stillness or moving toward it as winter approaches with its even more profound stillness. The haiga below, by Mary C. Taylor, is an obvious echo of Bashō's crow haiku. Consider the depiction of stillness in Taylor's haiga and in Bashō's crow haiga, described here by me:

twilight

a raven folds its wings

around darkness

In Bashō's haiga the haiku hangs in the air far above the scene as if to emphasize the extreme gravity of the haiga. In his stark drawing we find the crow on a dead branch. The bird's darkness is echoed by that of one of the branches. The bird is dwarfed by all the space above it and enclosed by two branches. All of these elements support the solemn stillness of the haiku. Mary C. Taylor's haiku is a bit figurative in its expression but creates the same mood as in Bashō's poem. Whereas Bashō's crow "settles" into the stillness, Taylor's raven "folds" that stillness into itself. In reality the raven is settling down for the night, which is near. The darkness that will soon come will all but make the stark black raven dissolve into it. Notice the broad-stroked patches of darkness sug-gestive of the raven's folding wings. Notice the somber expression on the raven's face. Overall, there is a pleas-ing parallel to the mood in Bashō's haiku and haiga in Mary C. Taylor's haiga.

winter moon...
undisturbed snow
on the cabin steps

Jeanne Emrich and Pamela Miller Ness have created moving haiga that also high-light stillness.

No one has been to the cabin since the snowfall in

Jeanne Emrich's haiga. The imagery of an empty dwelling in the woods at night is stark. But this is perhaps the place to which the author wants to return. The snow piled on the steps glows in the moonlight, almost encouraging the author to climb them and enter the cabin. The sketched-in ladder and the lighter gray, softly drawn mounds of snow on the steps perfectly capture a sense of stark but inviting stillness. The needlepoint haiga by Pamela Miller Ness evokes another kind of stillness. By chance one morning a rainbow had fallen across her blank journal page. She was probably about to put down her thoughts. Perhaps she was in a contemplative mood. The brilliantly colored rainbow of the original needlepoint represents the wonderful things that the artist will put down in the journal. If you have seen sunlight colored by a stained-glass window or turned into a rainbow by a glass prism you will have an idea of the quiet delight of this haiga.

Here is an example, this one by Carol Montgomery, of a more subtle incorporation of the verbal and visual elements of an eye-ku that deftly evokes stillness:

between pinches of goldfish food

stillness settles

The haiku's first and last lines tell what is happening in words. The five lines between, which are made up of seven dots—the particles of goldfish food—represent the water in the goldfish bowl. The words *stillness settles* are centered at the last line of the haiku and thus visually reflect the settling of the goldfish food at the bottom of the bowl.

CONCLUSION

To sum up, I would offer some advice to those who would like to try haiga. Develop a sense of the spatial relationship of haiku to drawing. Capture the essence of a haiku in your drawing. Emphasize suggestion rather than simple realistic representation. Try not to be too literal in your presentation of a haiku's imagery in general. Try your hand at simple nature sketches to accompany your haiku. Try illustrating some-one else's haiku. Try different mediums for your haiga—pencils, colored crayons, black grease pens, oil paints, watercolors, charcoal chalk, and even traditional sumi-e. Try your hand at a landscape. Try your hand at an abstract drawing and presentation. Try to cultivate simplicity and understatement. Try to do an "eye-ku." In general, whenever you are moved, write a haiku and make a sketch. Take a walk, then illustrate the haiku you came up with. Make time to sit down and do a painting or drawing of one of your own haiku. Finally, keep an alert eye out for those scenes in nature and in the people around you that will make a perfect haiga subject.

Creating with Others: Renga

SOME OF YOU may have played the game where a group of people sit in a circle and one person begins a story. At a certain point the person sitting to the right takes up the story by adding to what has already been said. Then the next person adds a little more, and so on. What a delight that was. Likewise, some of us may have played a circle game in which the first person whispers a sentence to the person sitting to his or her right. That person then whispers the message to the next person and so on. In the first game the delight comes from the impulsive way each person comes up with the next part of the story. In the second game the delight comes from seeing how much the original sentence changes by the time it reaches the last person. Renga, an overall term for a poem that is written with other people, is like these games. Its three main characteristics are spontaneity, improvisation, and fun. Spontaneity means that we do something without thinking too much about it, like taking a walk because it is sunny out. Improvisation means that we let our imagination go where it will, like some musicians do when they wander away from the main melody of a song and invent new variations and developments of the main tune. These two things lead to the third: fun.

CLASSICAL JAPANESE RENGA

Where did renga come from? It had its roots in the royal court of Japan, which organized renga writing parties. The poetry that resulted had the same formal elegance that we have seen in classical Japanese

tanka. A late example of this tradition is seen in these two linked
stanzas:

> as if I'd been caught
> by a sudden rain shower,
> dew on my sleeves
>
> both of us turn around to look
> on the path beneath the woods

—Matsunaga Teitoku

STRUCTURE AND CONTENT OF STANZAS

Notice that the stanzas are expressed in alternating short-long-short
and long-long stanzas. In Japanese these stanzas are, like most Japanese poetry, expressed in the 5-7-5 and 7-7 sound unit pattern. In the
first stanza the poet has dew on his sleeves. He may have merely leaned
over to look at some flowers and as he did so brushed against some
dew-covered plant. But traditionally dew was both a metaphor for tears
and a symbol of the short time of a human life. In any event the first
stanza has a moody sadness about it, perhaps even a tender thought
about how little time we may spend with our companions in our short
lives. This moodiness connects the second stanza to the first. The two
companions are on a long path through the woods. Something moves
them to look back at the same time. Perhaps they have wistful feelings
about leaving where they have been. It also again may reflect the same
sense of time passing that the dew symbolized. But such poetry could
also be humorous even if it still retained the bookish references to Chinese and Japanese culture that were part of the education of those at
court. Here is an example by an unknown author:

even in the middle of a dream
he seems to be suffering

asleep on a flower
the butterfly is pelted
by raindrops

The link between these two stanzas is a reference to a well-known self-contradictory story by the Chinese Taoist master Chuang-tze. In this story a man wakes up from a dream in which he had become a butterfly. Now that he is awake, the man wonders if he is indeed really a man or rather a butterfly that is only dreaming it is a man. There is something funny about the paradox of this story. If we didn't know the reference in these stanzas, we might think they were more serious than they are.

KASEN RENKU: THE THIRTY-SIX-STANZA RENGA FORM

Bashō wanted to avoid the too-refined elegance of traditional court renga and the too-earthy humor of the popular comic renga being written by his contemporaries. Instead, he retained humorous elements but connected them with an everyday realism. Bashō, who considered himself a better renga writer than haiku poet, perfected a thirty-six-stanza renga form. It is this shortened form of the hundred or more stanzas of court renga, renku, that came to be the central form of linked verse up to the present time. The style of renku is less full of the references and polish of court renga and more full of common speech and everyday activities. As an example of the thirty-six-stanza renku, or *kasen*, let us look at the first three stanzas of "Summer Moon," which Bashō composed with his friends. The first stanza was written by the Zen Buddhist priest Bonchō, with whom Bashō studied; the second stanza was by Bashō, and the third stanza was written by Kyorai, one of Bashō's disciples:

around the market
the smell of all these things!
the summer moon

"It's hot! It's so hot!"
voices say at every door

the second weeding
not completed, and already
buds on the rice

Notice how these three opening stanzas capture the recognizable feelings of summer. The first is filled with joy over the wonderful smells of the marketplace bustling in summer and the bright summer moon in a clear sky. Bashō links Bonchō by moving from the smells and sights of summer to the overall feeling of heat. We can easily visualize this scene. Many of us may have stood by a screen door or on a porch in summer hoping for a little breeze to relieve the sweltering heat. Kyorai moves the scene to the countryside, where a farmer is weeding. The conditions are so good that the rice has sprouted early. There is a sense of the vitality of nature in this scene. Many of us may remember looking at a garden that has become overly full of flowers almost overnight. The scene is like that. So we see that renga is organized by joining one stanza, or what is called a "link," to another by a related feeling.

Bashō created many ways to connect one link to another, but his overall term was "linking by scent." By this he meant that there was some commonality, however indirect, that suggested a connection between two links. The connection between the first and second links of "Summer Moon" is the season itself, which is named in the first and depicted through its characteristic heat in the second. The third link connects the repetition of the phrase "It's hot!" with the repetition of weeding, although we also realize that we are in summer. So we see that renga provides a series of shifting little scenes in which one link is related to both the link before it and the link after it through some kind of connection or "scent." It is as if we are looking through a kaleidoscope that constantly shifts the pattern of what we see while retaining fragments of the same color in each or watching a slide show in which each slide is different but connected to some general theme. However, as we shall see, there are rules for writing renga and renku, including the idea that each link must in some way move in another thematic direction as well as connect with the previous link in some way.

TAN-RENGA

Take a look at the following tan-renga, a two-person poem that resembles a tanka. The first link is by Carol Purington and the second by Larry Kimmel:

small clouds
in a clear sky—also swallows
flying high

> all that I did today I did
> as if her eyes were on me

The first short-long-short link establishes a buoyant feeling through the clouds, bright sky, and high-flying swallows. The second long-long link shifts the mood of being caught up in a beautiful day to one of specific familiarity and the human realm. Perhaps the author is guilty about something he did and knows that his companion or someone he respects would disapprove of it. Or perhaps he was doing something all day that would make someone proud of him. At any rate, the shift from the first to the second link is obvious and creates a self-contained little charge of feeling connecting these two little dramatic scenes. Here is another modern American tan-renga. Its first link is by Paul O. Williams and is followed by a link by Michael Dylan Welch:

morning sun—
all the patio tables
shining with new rain

church bells
church bells

Notice how the first link here, like the first link in the previous tan-renga, resembles haiku. Both could in fact be considered a more or less successful haiku. But a main point of linking poetry is to have the first link provide a strong base for the links that follow, for reasons we shall soon discuss. Notice how the connection in both links here is extremely optimistic if not ecstatic. The first link creates the image of a glorious day with all sorts of promise—the sun is shining and everything is glistening with fresh rain, as if, to stretch the imagery, newly baptized. The second link carries this mood into a more specific image of affirmation through purely sound imagery by repeating the phrase "church bells," as if the actual bells are repeating their tone. Perhaps it is Sunday morning and the bells are calling people to worship. Perhaps someone is getting married and the bells are announcing this joyous event. Whatever the occasion, we feel the jubilant nature of both links.

STRUCTURE AND RULES OF THE KASEN RENKU

Let us now look more closely at the structure of the kasen renku, the most widely practiced form of linked verse in America. Renku are often published to reflect their three-part division: an opening of six links (the front), the development in two pages of twelve links each (back and front), and a rapid-paced conclusion of six links (the back). In this thirty-six-link poem, the first link is all important. When renga were originally composed in Japan—at renga parties—the first link, or *hokku*, was written by one of the guests as a compliment to the host. It referred to the season in which the renga was taking place as well as the setting, thus grounding the renga as a whole. (It is this short-long-short verse form that became what we call haiku.). The second long-long link, or *wakiku*, was written by the host in response to the guest's subtle reference to the host's hospitality. The communal aspect of renga, which is described in a number of scenes in Bashō's *Narrow Path to the Interior*, continues by incorporating the other guests in alternating short-long-short and long-long links, none of which has the mandatory haikulike completeness of the hokku. In other words, there may be a sketchiness that highlights sound, dramatic imagery, or inflated, pure emotion in all the links except the hokku.

To prevent repetition, and thus to avoid a boring poem, the main organizing feature of renga is "link and shift," as we have described. In any three links the middle one could make a complete poem, say a tan-renga, with either the link before or after it. The linking by "scent" moves one link on to the other. The shifting of the focus in another direction in any link creates variety. In fact, the greater the shift, the greater the interest and excitement of a link. Another way to create variety and interest is to balance links on the activities of plants, animals, and nature in general with human activities. Still another method is the rule that all four seasons must be included in the links—spring and autumn, the most responded-to seasons in Japanese haiku, with from three to five links, and summer and winter, with one to three links. So, in addition to mentioning the current season in the hokku and wakiku, all seasons must appear at some point in the renga, making it a microcosm of the natural world.

In addition, there are three other special kinds of links. One is a moon link, which appears in the thirty-six-linked kasen renku at links five, thirteen, and twenty-nine. Since the seasonal calendar of Japan, like those of many early cultures, was organized on the phases of the moon, it is easy to understand the reason for the presence of moon links. Another is, specifically, the autumn moon, with its relation to harvest and the dramatic natural changes of this season. In fact, over the centuries in Japanese poetry and culture, the autumn moon has become an important symbol of the strong feelings provoked by the autumn season. Another special kind of link is the blossom or flower one, which in a kasen appears at links seventeen and thirty-five. In Japanese culture, flowers and tree blossoms are most usually identified with the cherry blossoms of spring. Spring and blossoms, a major topic of Chinese and Japanese art and poetry, naturally balance in their gaiety and promise the autumn harvest season and its symbol, the full autumn moon. A final special link considers love, usually the absence of one's companion, in pairs or in a small group somewhere in links seven through eighteen and nineteen through thirty. Traditional tanka has shown us the importance of this same topic.

EXAMPLES OF CONTEMPORARY KASEN RENKU

"Coast-to-Coast Renga" is an example of kasen-style renga. The ten authors of this work were: Joan Stamm (js), Bruce Ross (br), Rick Kuntz (rk), Jeff Witkin (jw), Tom Clausen (tc), Dee Evetts (de), David Bloch (db), Zeke Vayman (zv), Jim Kacian (jk), and Nancy Kline (nk). Here is that work. See if you can pick out the special kinds of links, and see how close to and how far from a traditional kasen renku it comes:

1   wet brown leaves   js
    trampled on the boardwalk
    Seattle morning

2   mallards on the autumn pond   br
    so loud beyond the rushes

3   he turns down the radio   rk
    then carves a frown
    into the pumpkin

4   a wedge of geese   jw
    slices the sunset

5 pizza shop   tc
   off the moonlit interstate
   break from drifting snow

6 spare pillows piled up   de
   on the bedside chair

7 sitting ovation   db   19 freshly tarred street   js
   for our pilot's soft landing   paw prints
   zero visibility   across the carpet

8 falling into the cloud   zv   20 the pigs almost lost   br
   Niagara Falls   in the dried-out weeds

9 spots on my glasses   jk   21 under the table   jw
   the multiple haloes   toes tunnel through
   of the well-lit park   its fur

10 cathedral windows   js   22 snow etching all the cracks tc
   glittering with saints   in the road heading out

11 sparkling stream . . .   br   23 after the holidays   de
   up and down the gorge's sides   a flock of sparrows
   car shadows   in the unsold trees

12 intravenous drip   jw   24 Weight Watchers   nk
   in and out of coma   self-portrait in her journal

13 mist lifts   tc   25 figures bouncing   db
   from the sodden hills   around the room-mirrors
   across the tracks   offered at auction

14 a hazy moon   de   26 a fruit sorbet   jk
   illuminates their rendezvous   at intermission

15 beneath flowering plum   nk
   they bury the past
   to watch the sun rise

16 farmers setting   db
   fields afire

17 road where you died   zv
   heavy in cane smoke
   and bougainvillea

18 the perfumed air   jk
   above Molasses Run
   the strawberry blonde

27 the strawberry blonde   js
   leans against the wall and whispers
   je suis fatigueé!

28 French Canadian border   br
   the Messier Apartments

29 on the window ledge   jw
   light from the tip
   of the moon

30 off to Never Never Land   tc
   Peter flies out of sight

31 in the mailbox   de
   another sweepstakes hype—
   you have been chosen

32 no postage necessary   nk
   she tosses the bottle into the sea

33 with snow-melt,   db
   what a splash they make—
   calls of returning songbirds

34 jaywalking   zv
   to the sunny side

35 in the hollow   jk
   of a footstep
   first crocus

36 within arms reach   js
   stand of pussy willows

The first thing you notice about this collaborative renku is the excitement of seeing so many different kinds of things connected with each other, many of them taken from the activities of our daily lives: carving a Halloween pumpkin, a pizza shop, a plane landing in zero visibility, Niagara Falls, farmers setting their fields on fire, pigs hidden in the weeds, Weight Watchers, Peter Pan, a sweepstakes announcement, jaywalking, and a first spring flower in a footprint! How could all these things fit together in one story? Of course they can't, and that is the special nature of renga. Renga and renku in particular do not have a narrative structure. They are not like haibun because they do not tell a story. The only hint of a story might occur in a small group of links on seasons, as in "Summer Moon," or on love. Because we constructed this renku through the mail, we only saw one link at a time and therefore could not create a narrative beyond the link of "scent." In fact, in all the renga parties in which I have participated, it was stressed that you should only be concerned with the link before yours. This is the magic of renga. When it is read or listened to it is like switching back and forth in no particular order between thirty-six television channels and observing what you see for only a split second. Part of the fun is seeing how the authors made their connection with the preceding link and how they went off in a different direction. Most of us will recognize the many references or allusions in this renga, for example, Never Never Land or Niagara Falls. But unless we knew French we might not see the pun in Messier Apartments. In an English pronunciation these apartments seem to be more untidy than any other apartments around, which wouldn't help renting them out. But in a French pronunciation the final "er" in Messier is pronounced like a long "a" as in "say." Also knowing French would help translate "je suis fatigueé" as "I am tired." Otherwise we should have no problem understanding and enjoying each link and the surprisingly swift and dramatic changes from one link to another. We notice that the hokku, or first link, takes place in autumn, as does the second. We can pick out moon links, blossom links, other seasonal links, and love links. And we can see that this renku ends in the traditional manner, with spring, in order to conclude on an upbeat note. But perhaps the traditional subjects do not fall exactly in the prescribed places, and perhaps there is a too obvious repetition of images. Nonetheless, it is quite imaginative and exciting and, of course, fun.

Here is another contemporary renku, "remaining snow." It was written by Carol Purington, who wrote the first link, and Raffael de Gruttola, who responded with the second link and every other link. See if you can pick out the traditional elements—the moon, blossoms, the seasons, love links, and an ending in spring. See if you can discover how one link connects to the next link. I should mention, however, that there is a reference to a children's book that many adults read as children but which is now considered inappropriate. The link's author is not intending to be offensive but is merely reminiscing about her childhood. Here is the renku:

1 remaining snow   cp
   . . . the red squirrel's tunnel
   roofless

        2 crocus buds   rdg
            where the elm branch rests

3 gusty wind
   the child and her kite
   against the sky

        4 on a thin wire
            the paper angel vibrates

5 calculus class
        —figuring when earth's shadow
   will halo the moon

6 the brilliance of Hale-Bopp
   at sundown

7 radiation ripples
   above the pond—
   sound of the hummingbird

   8 not to frighten the fireflies
      she whispers

9 chiaroscuro.
   wild turkeys
   walk the golf course

   10 sketching the lighthouse
      because it's there

11 on the saltmarsh
   broken sea shells
   leave with the tide

   12 two sets of footprints
      one sand castle

13 argument—
   how to decorate
   the nursery

   14 returning home
      Minnie Mouse in her arms

15 street dance
   —loudspeaker rhythm rises
   with the moon

19 at every station
   remembrance of things past—
   young boys play soccer

   20 physics lab demo
      on momentum

21 that nimbus cloud
   passing over . . .
            President's speech on race

   22 this tattered copy
      of "Little Black Sambo"

23 out of exile
   the gray hairs of a nest
   under the eaves

   24 at last enough rain
      to end the dry spell

25 only a few beans growing
   . . . the theology
   of weeds

   26 after the downpour
      spider mends his universe

27 all that racket
   —only a big frog
   in a small puddle

16 for his birthday
   lily of the valley and cognac

17 suddenly
   with the smell of new mown hay
   someone else somewhere else

18 in from the field
   horses carry the yellow sky

28 nowhere for the
   diving beetle to feed

29 on the pantry shelf
   an old glass pie plate—
   in three pieces

30 poison sumac rashes
   after apple picking

31 solitary Sojourner
   tracks dust . . .
   its robotic arms

32 just me and the night
   and a million crickets

33 by the campfires
   near the church the gypsies
   sing till dawn

34 you already so far away
   that wide-eyed moment

35 wind rattles the leaves . . .
   in the reflecting pool
   the rainbow comes and goes

36 to hold on to the notes
   of the nameless bird

Did you notice the references to the comet Hale-Bopp, a physics experiment on momentum, a nimbus cloud, or the satelite Sojourner? Did you know that "chiaroscuro" is an Italian word for the light and shade effect in a painting? Did you see the joke in link twenty-nine on the pie? Was there something amusing about the connection between links thirteen and fourteen? Have you ever experienced a night like the one described in link thirty-two?

THE TWENTY-LINK *NIJUIN*

A shorter version of the kasen renku is the twenty-link nijuin. I have used the nijuin while discussing linked verse in workshops on haiku for two reasons. One is that it is short enough to comfortably point out all its renga features in the limited time of a workshop. The other is that because it is short, when there is an attempt to write one, the participants in the workshop are less often "put on the spot." Like the kasen, the nijuin has a hokku with a reference to the season in its first short-long-short link and a long-long second link wakiko, or response, that also mentions the season. There are moon and love links, and all the seasons are introduced as in a kasen, only less often. Here is an example of a nijuin I have often used in workshops. Entitled "Another Painting," this nijuin won the 1996 Haiku Society of America Renku Contest. Its two authors are John Stevenson, who composed the second link and every other link after that, and Ion Codrescu, the well-known Romanian haiku poet and sumi-e painter. See if you can identify the more obvious elements of traditional linked verse:

> first snow—   ic
> they put another painting
> in the living room
>
>   common weeds   js
>   encased in ice

lifting the stone
its pattern
on the ground

her hair in curls
reading a novel

harvest moon
counting each
train

waiting for a lover
the Milky Way

geese
just two of them
this time

Beethoven quartet
softly heard

at the bottom
of the bottle
dark sediments

through the window
smell of plum brandy

chipmunks
racing around
garbage cans

for a while the moon
in the swimming pool

long story
the pasta
gets overcooked

    the Marilyn cards
    out of shelf

salmon
a bear's mouthful
of eggs

    fixing the walls
    of the cabin

over the roof
the smoke goes
straight up

    melt off meanders
    through a parking lot

in the distance
blossoming orchard
and then the village

    a warm breeze
    turns the weather vane

Did you notice how, in comparison to the two kasen, "Another Painting" has an overall softer tone, with less intricate links and shorter line lengths? This makes it a good example to work with. Have you ever seen the luminous band of the Milky Way on a clear night? Have you heard or seen a long train going by or heard a Beethoven string quartet? Have you ever got to talking so much you forgot about your dinner? Do you know who Marilyn Monroe is and why there would be cards with her picture on them? Were you moved by the image of weeds coated with ice or surprised by the appearance of the bear?

NEW AMERICAN FORMS

Renrepeat

Renku can be fun to do; yet, as you can see, they demand a lot of attention to ensure that the many necessary elements of the form are not overlooked. In response to the perhaps complicated factors involved in putting a renku together, many American poets who were interested in linking verse created new forms of this kind of poetry. One of these is a six-line poem that was developed by Francine Porad, Marlene Mountain, and Kris Kondo. Here is an example of what they have called "renrepeat." Notice that, unlike renku, this form connects each line to the next by the same theme, in this case "repetition":

these days i don't always know if i've repeated myself	mm
for cryin' out loud I wish he'd get a hearing aid	fp
yesyesyesyesyesyesyesyesyesyesyesyesyesyesyesyes	kk
linked forms still a confusion with word repetition	mm
Fourth of July same guests and barbecue menu as last year	fp
déjà vu cousins chattering the short night into dawn	kk

These lines resemble haiku or senryu one-liners but are expressed in a conversational phrasing of everyday speech. You can see how much fun the authors had in putting their poem together. Can you identify the repeating element in each line?

Tan-renga Senryu

Another innovation is a tan-renga senryu. Here is one entitled "reverberations" by Francine Porad and Lesley Einer:

Confucius says: fp
   top of the ladder nice place—
      let's aim high

      so true . . .   le
      but remember Humpty Dumpty

Here the tan-renga form is turned into a vehicle for a joke responded to by another joke. The first link's first two lines is like a fortune cookie fortune that offers a figurative comment on success. The third line, with the author's tongue in her cheek, develops that figurative expression. The first line of the second link sounds as if it is seriously considering the advice of link one but then makes fun of the figurative expression through an allusion to the nursery rhyme character Humpty Dumpty.

Renbun and Renkay

In terms of American innovation of the linking poem, we should discuss the difference between developmental linking and sequencing. One new kind of developmental linking, in which one person's writing is responded to by a piece of writing by another person, is what Kenneth Leibman called "renbun." Here a haibun by one author is connected to a haibun by another author through some link of correspondence such as mood or image. Rich Youmans and Margaret Chula have been most active in experimenting with this kind of linking. Another kind of linking, perfected by Tom Tico and Patricia Neubauer, is to write a haibun in response to the mood or feeling of someone else's haiku. A final kind of developmental linking is a form developed by Helen K. Davie, which is called "renkay." In this five-stanza linked poem the first haiku stanza relates to spring, the second to summer, the third to autumn, and the fourth to winter. The last stanza is a senryu. The haiku and senryu are usually chosen from previously published works of a given author, so the author in this case is in fact linking himself or herself. But unlike other developmental forms, renkay is organized around a common theme. Here is an example with a San Francisco–area setting by Fay Aoyagi:

Palm Sunday—
riding a cable car
to a pancake restaurant

practicing Portuguese
each time I buy
ginger-flavored ice cream

E-business meeting
my eyes on colored leaves
dancing outside

bitter morning—
left in the parking lot
a trio of midget trees

North Beach pizzeria
a couple busy talking
to their own cellular phones

We can see how the fundamental necessity of including links on all four seasons in traditional linked verse structures this poem. We can also see the pattern of linking from one stanza to the next all within the context of scenes familiar to the San Francisco area: a food link between one and two, a communication link of speaking Portuguese in two and conducting electronic business in three, an exterior link of the autumn leaves in three and the parking lot trees in four, and a final stanza that recapitulates or repeats all the other links on food, communication, and an external scene in the concluding senryu of two people talking on phones at an outdoor beach pizzeria.

Sequences

In addition to this interest in developmental linking there has been an extensive use of sequencing in haiku-related poetry. We have seen how a group of haiku on a similar topic can be organized into a sequence. This could also be done with senryu, haibun, and tanka, and, in fact, there are examples in American haiku-related poetry of all of these. David Rice has created a special innovation of the sequence format in a book of what he calls "North American life-cycle tanka." Each of the five tanka in each individual sequence chronologically offers five different stages of life from childhood to adulthood. As an example, let us look at "Snow":

> as mom calls
> I pretend not to hear
> sled down the hill
> and just miss the tree
> one last time

> we were singing
> with the radio
> before the skid
> now I hear how quietly
> snow falls at night

> cold winter morning
> I stare at the snow
> on a distant peak
> and rehearse my divorce speech
> one last time

> late spring hike
> the trail still full of snow
> on the north slope
> we take turns walking
> in each other's footsteps

one patch of snow
full of pine needles
is all that's left
of the blizzard that howled
while we kissed

This sequence is linked by the season of winter and particularly its snow, which is named in every stanza but the first, where the sledding implies it. Can you tell what period in a person's life each tanka represents? Notice how, even as a sequence on winter experiences throughout the author's life, a hint of the impulse toward linking enters in: the movement of the sled links to the car's skid, the quiet snowfall links to the snow-covered distant mountain, the divorce speech contrasts with the couple walking in each other's footprints, and the trail covered by snow contrasts with the single patch of snow. As you can see, there is obviously a strong desire to connect one poem with another, whether with others or alone in poetry composition.

Rengay

By far the most widely practiced form of innovative American linked poetry is "rengay." This form was created by Garry Gay in 1992 primarily to allow poets to create a poem together even while they are, for example, taking a hike. But unlike renga, a rengay has a distinct, developed theme, and it limits its links to the season in which it occurs. So, in contrast to renga, a rengay, like a haibun, has a narrative development and tells a story. A rengay has six stanzas beginning with a short-long-short stanza, which is responded to by a long-long one. Stanzas three and four are short-long-short. Five is long-long, and the rengay concludes with another short-long-short stanza. In other words: 1-3, 2-2, 3-3, 4-3, 5-2, and 6-3. This form of verse is designed for two or three poets. A variation of the form, created by Michael Dylan Welch in 1993, simply alternates short-long-short and long-long stanzas beginning with a short-long-short one. In other words: 1-3, 2-2, 3-3, 4-2, 5-3, and 6-2. Here is an example of a rengay composed by

Rick Krivcher, Garry Gay, and John Thompson entitled "Friday the 31st." It is the end of the month and someone is moving, which is this rengay's theme. See how each author links to the previous stanza while still illustrating the common subject of moving:

moving day: rk
inside an empty box
the smell of rice cakes

                    down the musty hall   gg
                    spaces where pictures hung

luring our cat   jt
into the open van—
tuna sandwich

                    bare closet   rk
                    a whiff of aged leather

autumn wind—   gg
left on the kitchen counter
incense ashes

                    the landlord's beer breathed grunt   jt
                    as I hand him the keys

Did you notice how this lively rengay is linked together by the sense of smell? Individual connections, like the empty box of one with the bare spaces on the wall in two, depend on experiences of emptiness and confinement. Notice that this rengay is structured on the alternating short-long-short and long-long pattern.

Here is an example of the first rengay pattern, in which stanzas one, three, four, and six are in the short-long-short form. Called "breaking through," its two authors are Connie Meester and Valorie Broadhurst

Woerdehoff. The imagery and linking are more subtle and interior than that in "Friday the 31st." See if you can find what theme holds this rengay together and how the title relates to that theme:

shortest day of the year   cm
the slick road
between us

                        waiting with her   vbw
                        the cold starting in her feet

along that shallow stream   cm
one orchid
breaks through snow

ice melts   vbw
old couple walking
his hand warms in her pocket

                        leaving violets   cm
                        in her discarded journal

sunlight through clouds   vbw
just ahead
. . . the rain

This rengay captures the end of winter and the beginning of spring, the title's breakthrough into new life that is symbolized by the orchid. The poem is also divided into stanzas of utter coldness and separation in one and two, the breakthrough stanza of the beginning of spring in three, and stanzas of close companionship, colorful flowers, and warmth in four, five, and six. See if you can find how the individual links connect with each other.

Another and final example is in the same structural form with short-long-short links at stanzas one, three, four, and six. Like "Friday the 31st," its theme and development are direct and easy to follow. "Faint Rustle of Envelopes" was written by D. Claire Gallagher and Ebba Story:

> the postman's shoe print   dcg
> on a magnolia petal
>   news of her death

> faint rustle of envelopes   es
> through the slot in my door

> today's delivery . . .   dcg
> vacation airline tickets
> atop the Visa bill

> bedridden   es
>   the exotic landscape
>   on a German stamp

> here, on my cluttered desk   dcg
> the letter I never mailed

> my dashed-off thoughts—   es
> cool handle on the mail box
> under scattered stars

With a little thought we can see how one stanza links to the previous stanza, such as vacation tickets with the exotic German landscape. But there is also a subtle development of the theme of how communication through mail somehow distances us from lived experiences. Because of this there is a kind of moodiness that colors each of the links of this fine rengay. Notice how it concludes on a sensitive and affirmative note in which this hovering mood of separation is reversed in the beauty of the distant stars.

CONCLUSION

To sum up I would offer some advice if you would like to write linked poetry with others. Don't let the somewhat complex structure of a kasen renku scare you away. Make a worksheet of its form and designate the appropriate special function of each link. Then get together and have fun writing one. Try your hand at tan-renga and American innovations in linked verse poetry like one-line renga, senryu tan-renga, renbun, linked tanka, renkay, and, especially, rengay. Try to write a nijuin renku like "Another Painting." Take a walk with one or two friends and compose a rengay on a theme that reflects your experience that day. Practice writing a good hokku that will hold a renga together. Practice with the structural device of "link and shift." Remember that any three adjacent lines of a renga should make up a complete link, so, except for the hokku, each link connects with the last lines of the preceding stanza and the first lines of the following stanza to produce two acceptable links. Linking may be done in many ways. Don't forget that you can link by contrast as well as association. Be especially careful not to exactly repeat an image or phrase. Remember to include a balance of persons, places, and things in your renga. Remember some of your links should be based on a subtle correspondence of mood, so don't overdo the obvious when you link. Also remember that the more extreme the shift is from one link to the next the better. After all, we are looking for variety and interest in the progression of a renga. In other words, use your imagination to the fullest when writing linked verse with others.

Further Notes on Haiku Form

MODERN AMERICAN HAIKU takes two general forms. One is the "traditional" form. Here, the first line generally connects with a large, more generalized aspect of nature. Line one is usually separated from lines two and three by a punctuation mark, thus setting up a juxtaposition between line one and the concrete image developed in lines two and three. There is often a higher tone in the word choice and phrasing. Also, lines two and three are often almost a grammatically correct sentence in their structure. Consider this example for these elements:

> Becoming dusk,—
>   the catfish on the stringer
>   swims up and down
>
> —Robert Spiess

The other general form of modern American haiku is "modern" in its presentation. Here the first line, as in "traditional" haiku, generally connects with a large, more generalized aspect of nature. End punctuation after the first line is, however, usually omitted, although an implicit break is often clearly intended. In this way, a juxtaposition is set up between line one and lines two and three where a concrete image is developed. The biggest difference between the two forms is the manner in which each phrases its lines. In "modern" haiku there is a tendency to organize lines two and three in short, conversational phrasing. A more direct, less formal tone is produced through this phrasing. Look for this tone in the following example:

> winter sun
> a stranger makes room
> without looking
>
> —John Stevenson

But, of course, there are many variations on these two basic approaches to haiku form. Some modern American haiku place the generalized connection with nature on the third line and their punctuation at the end of the second line or the beginning of the third line, developing the concrete image in lines one and two. Some haiku imply the connection to broader nature somewhere in the three lines that develop the single image of the given haiku. Here are examples of each:

> carrying home
> a jar of mint—
> summer moon
>
> —Gloria Procsal

> until we stop
> the long straight backbone
> of the heron
>
> —Bruce Ross

There are also many variations to the straight left margin for the three lines of a haiku, with the stair-step indentation in reverse favored by many of the important early American haiku poets, as in the Spiess catfish haiku, being the most common.

A closer look at the ways in which haiku lines are presented on a page might be helpful. Here are two minimalist haiku in which the fewest possible words make up the poem. The first one, by Cor van den Heuvel, may be related to eye-ku in that the single word *tundra*, which is a treeless expanse of frozen land in the Arctic region, resembles on the page what it means.

tundra

                          séance
                          a white
                          moth

                          —Raymond Roseliep

What is gained and what is lost in the second haiku by using only four words to describe a gathering to speak to the dead that is juxtaposed to a white moth?

Many haiku are one-liners. Perhaps their authors are trying to capture the sense in which some Japanese haiku is written in a continuous line. What different effect do these one-liners have as opposed to their being written as typical three-liner haiku?

trying the old pump a mouse pours out

                          —Lee Gurga

smoke from a neighbor's chimney   loneliness

                          —Marlene Mountain

the old irrigation ditch   gathering in   autumn dusthaze

                          —Elizabeth Searle Lamb

Here are examples of two-liners. Could a better haiku have been written if a third line had been added? Are these two-line haiku different from a long-long link in a renga?

nightfall   so still . . .
  horse chestnuts hit the parked car   only the falling plum blossoms

      —Alan Pizzarelli   —Sarah Fitzjarrald

Here are examples of four-liners. Notice the visual effect created by adding a fourth line in each.

the river
        going over
the afternoon
going on

        —Dee Evetts

waterfall at night—
her long
        black
                hair

        —Charles D. Nethaway, Jr

Would expressing these haiku in three lines have the same effect?

Finally, here are examples of vertical haiku. Japanese haiku are written vertically. Perhaps those authors who write vertical haiku are trying to capture some quality of Japanese writing. Are there any other qualities that are special to vertical haiku?

no one
else
lives here—

new stem
on

the
lemon
tree

        —John Martone

midnight
lakeshore
names
    of
forgotten
    loves
painted
    on
    the
    rocks

        —Lee Gurga

Can you see the lemon tree and perhaps the stem in the shape of the first haiku? Can you see the shoreline in the right margin and the rocks jutting out into the lake in the left margin of the second haiku?

APPENDIX B

Taking a Walk: Ginko

THERE IS NO BETTER WAY to find inspiration for your haiku than by taking a walk in nature. If we slow down a little in such a setting wonderful things will begin to appear to us. Even if we are walking down a city street beneath the clouds or an open sky something wonderful is bound to happen. As I mentioned before, Japanese workers often take a break by going on such walks to be inspired and to write haiku. Such a walk is called a *ginko* in Japanese.

A traditional ginko has two parts. The first part is the actual walk on which haiku are composed. The second part is the selection of favorite haiku from all those composed. A small group of judges are selected for this job. The selection and judges' comments are called a *kukai* in Japanese. In American ginko all the haiku are often posted on a wall so everyone can read them before the kukai. It is really thrilling to see what others have responded to on the same walk you took. Sometimes someone else has seen and felt the exact same thing you have and composed a haiku on it. Sometimes we are delighted or surprised by a haiku on something we overlooked. In addition to such general haiku-writing walks, there are more specialized versions in Japan in which some natural phenomenon becomes a focal point for inspiration. One of these is viewing the full autumn moon, or *otsukimi*. In the autumns of 1998 and 1999, I led haiku writing at such an event sponsored by the Japan-America Society of Vermont. The participants were of all ages and included parents, children, teachers, students, and visitors from Japan. We all looked at the moon and wrote haiku on the experience. Then we stood under the moon and one by one recited our haiku.

There was something especially enjoyable about sharing our haiku inspirations in this natural setting.

What are my suggestions for taking a haiku walk? Perhaps, if you have friends who are interested in haiku, you could start a haiku club. I have belonged to several of these, and it was wonderful meeting once a month to read and discuss our haiku. Perhaps some fellow students who are interested in haiku can take a walk in a park together with the intention of composing haiku. A little notebook would be helpful. Get inspired by nature. Slow down and be patient. Something will touch you, and this will become your haiku. After your walk, share your haiku with each other. See which ones surprise you and which are clearly awesome. See if anyone came up with something amusing. Above all, enjoy yourself.

Further Notes on Haiku Aesthetics

WABI SUCHNESS IN HAIKU
BY H. F. NOYES

Wabi refers generally to the sort of poverty or simplicity of living where there is, through acceptance, a kind of contentment. "Suchness" refers to the seemingly ordinary things that surprise and reward us when we discover it as a welcome part of everyday life. "Nature is wont to hide itself," said Heraclitus in the fifth century B.C. Two hiding places are brought to light in these haiku of James W. Hackett:[1]

> The nameless flower
>   climbing this trail with me
>   is a yellow you can taste!

> Buildings hide the sky
>   and pavement the earth, yet
>   this week grew to seed.

There may be an aspect of redeeming humor along with the prosaic plainness of wabi:[2]

> Sometimes the oddest thing,
>   like this orange pip,
>   begs not to be thrown away.

Humble—even desolate—circumstances can be relieved by a sense of beauty:[3]

Red clouds glowing
at sunrise—reflected
in the pigsty mud

—Bruce Leming, original and translation

This haiku in its original, tremendously alive Scots tongue is:

Reid cluds lemin
at keek-o-day—refleckit
in the cray glaur

Though wabi is most often an *unexpected* recognition of the faithful
suchness of things and the beauty of the ordinary, here one feels no surprise on the part of the poet rooted to the earth and at home beneath
the heavens. I find the wabi element delightful in these two other farm
and garden haiku:[4, 5]

Summer dusk
—puddles
where the melons were

—Matthew Louvière

Envelope of seeds:
A flower like the picture
Will bloom, I hope so.

—Sakuzo Takada

Louvière is content to see things just as they are, to see "nothing
that is not there and nothing that is."[6] In Takada's haiku I cherish the
gentle humor, charm, and naïveté of the vernacular, in which the Japanese excel.

There is wabi in the simplest pursuits of our daily life, such as the
bread delivery or a saucepan's transfer in winter. How far the mundane
ordinary is transcended in the following:[7, 8]

daybreak—
from the bread truck's roof
frost swirls

—Tom Clausen

Carrying a saucepan
Over a little bridge in Yodo
Someone in the snow.

—Buson

The first has a powerful aura of *wu shih*—"nothing special." In the background, do I hear, "Give us this day our daily bread"? Buson's haiku offers a charming picture of life at its sweetest—"near the bone," as Thoreau put it. It depicts no one of note carrying nothing of any account nowhere that matters, and is redolent of the truest wabi. Robert Spiess, throughout his *noddy*, maintains a quality of humbleness that reveals the essential truth of things just as they are. In "Progress," his very language expresses wabi: "tumblebug / tumbling a dungball past / tumbly digs."[9] A kind word or a comfortable bench can bring moments of contentment even in a miserable life:[10, 11]

rushing out
  with more garbage!
genuine,
  the collector's
"thank you, sir"

—Robert Spiess

Small-town park:
he adjusts his spine
to the slatted bench.

—Dee Evetts

Issa is a poet often grounded in the earthiness of wabi. The following reflects his loyalty to the aesthetic philosophy of wu shih:[12]

The man pulling radishes
pointed the way
with a radish.

Examples of wabi can be beautiful, too, but the kind of beauty to be preferred is that formulated by Clement Hoyt as "an easy austerity."[13]

This is well illustrated in a haiku by Brett Peruzzi:[14]

> First frost—
> the icy beauty
> of a flower's last day

In one memorial issue for Raymond Roseliep we have a classic haiku of wabi—rare among so-called death poems. It takes us deeply into the silence and calmness that ensue when, through the perspective of a nature of detachment, a life is touched by grace:[15]

> wishing I were
> a dandelion
> I become one

THE HAIKU "MOMENT" AND ACCURACY
BY BRUCE ROSS

The American poet Elizabeth Bishop wrote somewhere in a notebook that what she values in poetry are: accuracy, spontaneity, and mystery.[16] Her poetry is recognized for the precise quality of her observations. I would like to appeal to this idea of accuracy in a discussion of the haiku "moment."

The international appeal of haiku lies in the accessible nature of the images that are its main structural feature. If the haiku works, at first reading, the images of that haiku should be objective, clear, and obvious. Without such values we have images that are too "airy," vague, and indefinite. To be true to the haiku "moment," at the first, we must be faithful to the determining images of that moment. Or, as the bard stated, "A rose by any other name would smell as sweet." But we must present that rose through our images and the expression of our images, notwithstanding the Heraclitean dictum that we can't step in the same river twice (or the Zennian turn that we can't step in the same river once). But, in the second place, there is subjectivity, the realm of our emotions and consciousness meeting the rose.

The problem of subjectivity as it affects our images in modern haiku may be approached by looking at the expression of sentiment in classical Japanese haiku. First, one by Issa:

> If you are tender to them,
> The young sparrows
> Will poop on you.[17]

And this one by Bashō:

> Mice in their nest
> Squeak in response
> To the young sparrows.[18]

We are reminded by these two haiku of Bashō's idea that "nature has no emotion, but it has life."[19] In these haiku we see the young sparrows pooping and we hear the young mice squeaking and the young sparrows peeping. The life of these creatures is objectively presented. But we also feel the tender sentiment generated in the poets by these particular kinds of liveliness. Such objectivity linked with tenderness is a difficulty for the modern Western haiku poet. First, we must avoid the "pathetic fallacy," projecting emotions onto nonhuman nature, or so some critics would have it. Then we must be mindful of the "objective correlative," finding external images to express our internal emotions. We also should be considerate of Husserl's idea *zu den Sachen*, to return to the existential things themselves (as opposed to the idea or abstraction, including verbal ones, of things) so that they may reveal themselves to us. So we are stuck in a meditating place between objectivity and subjectivity.

Are we capable of the sentiment of Issa and Bashō? Most attempts in modern English haiku seem almost to parody such emotion as sentimentality rather than sentiment, particularly when they echo Issa. This is because of what has been termed the "postmodern condition," which has so fragmented the self and the world outside the self that we are hard-pressed in this schizophrenic condition to find space or time to engage our consciousness with the "out there" reality. Therefore, "mental" haiku are so enticing, those "spots of time" that well up from our past experiences and imagined possible experience. But to say that this, and only this, is haiku is to throw the baby out with the bath water.

To answer the question, the most successful versions of Issalike and Bashōlike sentiment are reflected through the emotion of sabi, which, through objectivity and projected loneliness, evokes the poetic value of pathos. Look at this prize-winning haiku by Ebba Story as an example:

peeping . . . peeping
the lost duckling's wake
through evening shadows[20]

In the "postmodern condition," pathos may reflect, in a more existentially relevant way than sentiment, how we have sympathetic emotion for the nonhuman life around us and for the failing nature of the human condition.

We may, nonetheless, be accurate to our mental expression, and some current haiku poets have mastered such expression. Accuracy is not, at the other extreme, a mere representation of what is experienced, although the nature sketch is an accepted form in Japanese haiku. We also all edit and some even embellish our images (Bashō did) to create the best aesthetic effect from those images. But we are looking for images that engage our emotion in quite specific ways. We want to be open to the experience, to the realities of things, like Bashō's pine tree. But we want those realities to be evoked through certain emotional states, like wabi and sabi, that are in part generated by those very realities themselves. But to reach such "emotional" accuracy we must do the impossible: We must slow down, and like the little child at the street corner, we must stop, look, and listen.

1. J.W. Hackett, *The Zen Haiku and other Zen Poems of J. W. Hackett* (Tokyo: Japan Publications 1983), pp. 192 and 86.

2. Ibid., p.14.

3. Bruce Leeming, *Scots Haiku* (Linces, U.K: Hub Editions, 1995).

4. *Woodnotes* 17 (1993): 11.

5. *Wind Chimes* 25 (undated): p.4.

6. Wallace Stevens, "The Snow Man." *The Collected Poems of Wallace Stevens* (New York: Alfred A. Knopf, 1975), p. 9.

7. Tom Clausen, *Unraked Leaves* (Wellsville, N.Y.: Benson Smyth Publishing, 1995), p. l.

8. Translated by Edith Shiffert and Yuki Sawa.

9. Robert Spiess, *noddy* (Madison, Wis.: Modern Haiku Press, 1997), p. 35.

10. Ibid., p. 15.

11. *Wind Chimes* 27 (1989): 6 (in renga, "Four-for-a-dollar Goldfish").

12. Translated by Robert Hass, in *The Enlightened Heart*, ed. Stephen Mitchell (New York: Harper & Row, 1989), p. 99.

13. Clement Huyt, *Storm of Stars, The Collected Poems and Essays of Clement Hoyt* (Baton Rouge, La.: The Green World, 1976); cited by Tom Clausen, *South by Southeast* 4, no. 3 (1997): 22.

14. *Frogpond* 10, no. 4 (1987): 20.

15. *Wind Chimes* 11 (1984): 12.

16. Cited by J. D. McCatchy, "Letters from a Lonely Poet," rev. of Elizabeth Bishop, *One Art, Letters*, ed. by Robert Giroux (New York: Farrar, Strauss & Giroux, 1994), *The New York Times Book Review*, April 17, 1994, p. 23.

17. Translated by R. H. Blyth, *Haiku*, Vol. 2: Spring (Tokyo: Hokuseido Press, 1981), p. 526. (By permission.)

18. Ibid., p. 520. (By permission.)

19. Cited from Makoto Ueda by M. B. Duggan, "The Haiku as Weapon," *Raw NervZ Haiku* 1, no. 1 (Spring 1994): 7.

20. *Woodnotes* 20 (Spring 1994): 31. (By permission.)

Further Reading

SO, YOU HAVE NOW LEARNED a lot about haiku and its related forms and you want to read more. The following lists of individual collections, anthologies, journals, newspapers, Web sites, studies, and translations will help you do this. With a little assistance from a librarian you should be able to locate most of them. Some of them, however, because they were produced independently or by very small presses, will be harder to locate. After reading more about haiku and trying your hand at haiku and haikulike forms, you might wish to try to publish your own work in one of the journals, newspapers, or Web sites listed here. Remember that when you send a submission by mail you must include a self-addressed, stamped envelope (SASE) so that your work can be returned to you. Be sure to put your name and address on every sheet of work you submit. Be prepared to have to revise your work. But also be prepared for the thrill of publishing your first haiku.

GENERAL STUDIES AND SOURCES

Blyth, R. H. *HAIKU,* 4 vols. (Hokuseido, 1949–1952).

Bowers, Faubion. *The Classic Tradition of Haiku, An Anthology* (Dover, 1996).

Carter, Stephen D. *Traditional Japanese Poetry, An Anthology* (Stanford, 1991).

Henderson, Harold G. *Haiku in English* (Charles E. Tuttle, 1967).

———. *An Introduction to Haiku* (Doubleday, 1958).

Issa. *The Autumn Wind,* trans. Lewis Mackenzie (Kodansha, 1984).

Saigyō. *Mirror for the Moon*, trans. William R. Lafleur (New Directions, 1977).

Ueda, Makoto. *Matsuo Bashō* (Twayne, 1970).

International Anthologies

Haiku, Canadian Anthology, ed. Dorothy Howard and André Duhaime (Editions Asticou, 1985).

A Hidden Pond, Anthology of Modern Haiku, ed. Kôko Katô and David Burleigh (Kadokawa Shoten, 1997).

The Iron Book of British Haiku, ed. David Cobb and Martin Lucus (Iron Press, 1998).

Knots, The Anthology of Southeastern European Haiku Poetry, ed. Dimitar Anakiev and Jim Kacian (Prijatelj, 1999).

New Zealand Haiku Anthology, ed. Cyril Childs (New Zealand Poetry Society, 1993).

Red Moon Anthology, ed. Jim Kacian and others (Red Moon, 1996 and annually).

Wind in the Long Grass: A Collection of Haiku, ed. William J. Higginson (Simon & Schuster, 1991).

International Journals and Newspapers

Albatross, ed. Ion Codrescu (Romania)

Asaki Evening News, ed. David McMurray (Japan)

Blithe Spirit, ed. Caroline Gourlay (England)

· *Ko*, ed. Kôko Katô (Japan)

Mainichi Daily News, ed. Kazuo Sato (Japan)

Mirrors, ed. Jim Force (Canada)

Paper Wasp, ed. Janis Bostok (Australia)

Raw Nervz Haiku, ed. Dorothy Howard (Canada)

Shiki Internet Haiku Salon (online) (Japan)

Sparrow, ed. Marijan Čekolj (Croatia)

still, ed. ai li (England)

Woodpecker, ed. William Lofvers (The Netherlands)

HAIKU

American Haiku Anthologies

The Haiku Anthology, ed. Cor van den Heuvel (Norton, 1999).

Haiku Moment, An Anthology of Contemporary North American Haiku, ed. Bruce Ross (Charles E. Tuttle, 1993).

Midwest Haiku Anthology, ed. Randy Brooks and Lee Gurga (High/Coo, 1992).

The San Francisco Haiku Anthology, ed. Jerry Ball, Garry Gay, and Tom Tico (Smythe-Warthe, 1992).

Individual American Haiku Collections

Clausen, Tom. *Unraked Leaves* (Benson Smyth, 1995).

Dickson, Charles. *A Moon in Each Eye* (AHA, 1993).

Elliott, David. *Wind in the Trees* (AHA, 1992).

Gurga, Lee. *The Measure of Emptiness* (Press Here, 1991).

Hackett, J. W. *The Zen Haiku and Other Zen Poems of J. W. Hackett.* (Japan Publications, 1993).

Kenny, Adele. *At the Edge of the Woods* (Yorkshire House, 1997).

Lamb, Elizabeth Searle. *Casting into a Cloud, Southwest Haiku* (From Here, 1985).

Nutt, Joe. *Kernels* (Nutt Studio, 1989).

Porad, Francine. *The Patchwork Quilt* (Vandina, 1993).

Roseliep, Raymond. *Rabbit in the Moon* (Alembic, 1983).

Ross, Bruce. *Silence* (HMS, 1997).

Rotella, Alexis. *Voice of the Mourning Dove* (Jade Mountain, 1991).

Spiess, Robert. *The Shape of Water* (Modern Haiku, 1982).

Stevenson, John. *Some of Silence* (Red Moon, 1999).

Swist, Wally. *Unmarked Stones* (Burnt Lake, 1988).

Tico, Tom. *Spring Morning Sun* (Belltower, 1998).

van den Heuvel, Cor. *Dark* (Chant, 1982).

Virgil, Anita. *One Potato Two Potato Etc.* (Peak, 1991).

Virgilio, Nicholas A. *Selected Haiku* (Burnt Lake, 1988).

Wills, John. *Reed Shadows* (Burnt Lake, 1987).

Young, Virginia Brady. *Warming a Snowflake* (Sleeping Giant, 1990).

American Haiku Journals

Acorn, ed. A. C. Missias

Aha!, ed. Jane Reichhold (online)

Ant Ant Ant Ant Ant, ed. Chris Gordon

Chaba Haiku Journal, ed. John Hudak (online)

Frogpond, ed. Jim Kacian

Geppo, ed. Jean Hale

The Heron's Nest, ed. Christopher Herold (online)

Modern Haiku, ed. Robert Spiess

The Nor'easter, ed. Larry Rungren

South by Southeast, ed. Stephen Addiss

Tundra, ed. Michael Dylan Welch

SENRYU

General Studies and Translations

Blyth, R. H. *Japanese Life and Character in Senryu* (Hokuseido, 1960).

———. *Senryu, Japanese Satirical Verses* (Hokuseido, 1949).

Senryu: Poems of the People, ed. J. C. Brown (Charles E. Tuttle, 1991).

Ueda, Makoto. *Light Verse from the Floating World* (Columbia, 1999).

American Anthologies

Fig Newtons, Senryu to Go, ed. Michael Dylan Welch (Press Here, 1993).

Individual American Collections

Evetts, Dee. *endgrain* (Red Moon, 1997).

Montgomery, Carol. *Starting Something* (Los Hombres, 1992).

Pizzarelli, Alan. *The Flea Circus* (Islet, 1989).

Porad, Francine. *Ladles and Jellyspoons* (Vandina, 1996).

Rotella, Alexis. *Looking for a Prince* (White Peony, 1991).

Sheirer, John. *Home Sick From Work* (First Blade, 1996).

American Journals and Newsletters

Frogpond

Haiku Headlines, A Monthly Newsletter of Haiku and Senryu, ed. David Priebe

Modern Haiku

HAIBUN

Studies and Translations

Bashō. *The Narrow Road to the Deep North*, trans. Nobuyuki Yuasa (Penguin, 1966).

Issa. *The Spring of My Life*, trans. Sam Hamill (Shambhala, 1997).

Japanese Poetic Diaries, ed. Earl Miner (University of California, 1969).

American Anthologies

Journey to the Interior, American Versions of Haibun, ed. Bruce Ross (Charles E. Tuttle, 1998).

Individual American Collections

Easter, Charles. *Spirit Dancer* (Black Bough, 1997).

Kacian, Jim. *Six Directions: Haiku of the Local Ecology* (La Alameda, 1997).

Lynch, Tom. *Rain Drips from the Trees: Haibun along the Trans-Canadian Highway* (self-published, 1992).

Neubauer, Patricia. *Foxes in the Garden and Other Prose Pieces* (self-published, 1993).

Schmidt, Paul F. *Temple Reflections* (Hummingbird, 1980).

tripi, vincent. *Haiku Pond: A trace of the trail . . . and Thoreau* (Vide, 1987).

American Journals

American Haibun and Haiga, ed. Jim Kacian and Bruce Ross

Black Bough, ed. Charles Easter

Frogpond

Modern Haiku

TANKA

Studies and Translations

Konkinshu, A Collection of Poems Ancient and Modern, trans. Laurel Rasplica Rodd (Cheng & Tsui, 1996).

Ueda, Makoto. *Modern Japanese Tanka* (Columbia, 1996).

American Anthologies

Footsteps in the Fog, ed. Michael Dylan Welch (Press Here, 1994).

Tanka Splendor (AHA, annually to 1999, then online).

Wind Five Folded, ed. Jane and Werner Reichhold (AHA, 1994).

Individual American Collections

Clausen, Tom. *A Work of Love* (Tiny Poems, 1997).

Conforti, Gerard John. *Now that the Night Ends* (AHA, 1996).

Little, Geraldine. *More Light, Larger Vision* (AHA, 1992).

Rice, David. *In Each Other's Footsteps* (Pressed for Time, 1996).

Reichhold, Jane and Werner. *In the Presence Tanka* (AHA, 1998).

Shelley, Pat. *Turning My Chair* (Press Here, 1997).

Tanemura, Kenneth. *No Love Poems* (Small Poetry, 1994).

American Journals

American Tanka, ed. Laura Maffei

Hummingbird, ed. Phyllis Walsh

Lynx: A Journal for Linking Poets, ed. Jane and Werner Reichhold

HAIGA

Studies and Practice

Addiss, Stephen. *Haiga: Takebe Socho and the Haiku-Painting Tradition* (University of Hawaii, 1995).

Franck, Frederick. *Zen Seeing, Zen Drawing* (Bantam, 1995).

Momiyama, Nanae. *Sumi-e: An Introduction to Ink Painting* (Charles E. Tuttle, 1967).

Okamoto, Naomi. *Japanese Ink Painting: The Art of Sumi-e* (Sterling, 1995).

Ueda, Makoto. *The Path of Flowering Thorn: The Life and Poetry of Yosa Buson* (Stanford, 1998).

Zolbrod, Leon M. *Haiku Painting* (Kodansha, 1982).

Individual American Collections

Emrich, Jeanne, and Susan Frame. *Barely Dawn* (Lone Egret, 1999).

Mountain, Marlene. *nature talks back* (self-published, 1994).

Rozmus, Lidia. *Twenty Views from Mole Hill* (Deep North, 1999).

Amy Zenner and Jessie Spicer Zenner, *Zen ABC,* (Charles E. Tuttle, 1993).

American Journals

American Haibun and Haiga

bamboo forest, ed. Rodrigo de Siquiera (online)

HAIGA online, ed. Jeanne Emrich

RENGA

Studies

Miner, Earl. *Japanese Linked Poetry* (Princeton, 1979).

Sato, Hiroaki. *One Hundred Frogs: From Renga to Haiku to English* (John Weatherhill, 1983).

American Collections

Conti-Entin, Carol, Helen K. Davie, Cherie Hunter Day, D. Clair Gallagher, Marianna Monaco, Ce Rosenow, Ebba Story, and Joan Zimmerman. *Beyond Within, A Collection of Rengay* (Sundog, 1997).

Colon, Carlos, and Alexis Rotella. *sassy* (Tragg, 1998).

Gay, Garry, and Michael Dylan Welch. *Four Rengay* (self-published, 1999).

Kondo, Kris, Marlene Mountain, and Francine Porad. *Other Rens* (Vandina, 2000).

Mountain, Marlene, and Francine Porad. *cur*rent* (Vandina, 2000).

Reichhold, Jane, and others. *Narrow Road to Renga* (AHA, 1989).

Round Renga Pond, ed. Jane Reichhold (AHA, 1990).

American Journals

Chameleon (online)

Frogpond

Lynx, A Journal of Linking Poets

WRITING ABOUT HAIKU

Noyes, H. F. *Favorite Haiku*, 4 vols. (Red Moon, 1998–2000).

Spiess, Robert. *New and Selected Speculations on Haiku* (Modern Haiku, 1988).

tripi, vincent. *tribe* (Swamp, 1995).

Permissions

The following abbreviations have been used.

A   *Acorn*

AHH   *up against the window: American Haibun and Haiga*, ed. Jim Kacian and Bruce Ross (Red Moon, 1999)

AHH2   *stone frog: American Haibun and Haiga*, ed. Jim Kacian and Bruce Ross (Red Moon, 2001)

AT   *American Tanka*

BS   *Brussels Sprout*, ed. Francine Porad

F   *Frogpond*

FN   *Fig Newtons, Senryu to Go*, ed. Michael Dylan Welch (Press Here, 1993)

HI   *Haiku International*, ed. Kazuo Sato and others

HO   *HAIGA online*

I   *Inkstone*, ed. Keith Southward and Marshall Hryciuk

L   *Lynx, A Journal for Linking Poets*

MH   *Modern Haiku*

NC   *New Cicada*

n.p.   no publisher

OR   *Other Rens*, by Kris Kondo, Marlene Mountain, and Francine Porad (Vandina, 2000)

P   *Persimmon*, ed. Mary C. Taylor

PJL   *Point Judith Light*, ed. Patrick Frank

RMA   *Red Moon Anthology*, ed. Jim Kacian and others (Red Moon, 1996 and annually)

SXSE   *South by Southeast*

T   *Tidepool*, ed. Herb Barrett

TS   *Tanka Splendor*

TT   *The Trees*, by Bruce Ross (Plowman, 1991)

twst   *thousands of wet stones*, by Bruce Ross (M.A.F., 1988)

u.p.   unpublished

W   *Woodnotes*, ed. Michael Dylan Welch

WFF   *Wind Five Folded*, ed. Jane and Werner Reichhold (AHA, 1994)

I have made every attempt to contact the author, artist, or copyright holder of the work cited in this book and would appreciate hearing from any author, artist, or copyright holder not so contacted.

Stephen Addiss: "old pond *sumi-e*" and "birthday snow *sumi-e*" u.p.; by permission of the artist.

Nasira Alma: "first snow drawing," SXSE 4, no. 3 (1997).

Kay F. Anderson: "just as it is haiga," SXSE 4, no. 3 (1997); by permission of the artist.

Fay Aoyagi: "Third Home," u.p.; by permission of the author.

Cathy Drinkwater Better: "amaryllis," AHH; by permission of the author.

Mary Lou Bittle-DeLapa: "weeding the garden," TS (1999); by permission of the author.

Oliver K. Blackburn: "convalescence," MH 28, no. 1 (1997); by permission of the author.

David Bloch: "Coast-to-Coast Renga," u.p.; by permission of the author.

David Carlson: "worrying," F 22, no. 3 (1999); by permission of the author.

Yu Chang: "a mountain road," F 20, no. 2 (1996); by permission of the author.

Cyril Childs: "Pantry Shelf," F 22, no. 1 (1999); by permission of the author.

Emma Clausen: "outside," MH 29, no. 1 (1998); by permission of the author.

Tom Clausen: "our director," MH 26, no. 2 (1995); "this being human," TS (1999); "I look over," *A Work of Love* (Tiny Poems, 1997); "side by side" and "Coast-to-Coast Renga," u.p.; by permission of the author.

Ion Codrescu: "Another Painting Renku," F 20, no. 1 (1997); by permission of the author.

L. A. Davidson: "when the owner comes," MH 30, no. 2 (1999); by permission of the author.

Cherie Hunter Day: "watching," AT 6 (1999); by permission of the author.

Raffael de Gruttola: "in the house plants," BS 9:2 (1992); "remaining snow renku," F 22, no. 1 (1999); by permission of the author.

Charles Dickson: "out of the fog bank," BS 6, no. 2 (1989); "migrating geese," MH 20, no. 1 (1989); by permission of Virginia P. Dickson.

Lesley Einer: "reverberations tan-renga," L (May 96); by permission of the author.

David Elliott: "among leafless trees," PJL 1, no. 1 (1992); by permission of the author.

Jeanne Emrich: "winter moon *sumi-e*," AHH; by permission of the artist.

Robert Epstein: "dermatologist's office," F 22, no. 1 (1999); by permission of the author.

Judson Evans: "Haibun for Dennis: December 12, 1994," *Hands Full of Stars* (Aether, 1995); by permission of the author.

Dee Evetts: "channel dispute," F 22, no. 3 (1999); "last grandchild," *endgrain* (Red Moon, 1997); "Coast-to-Coast Renga," u.p.; "the river," *A Small Ceremony* (From Here, 1988); by permission of the author.

Carol Field: "through falling snow," MH 31, no. 1 (2000); by permission of the author.

Sarah Fitzjarrald: "so still…" MH 22, no. 1 (1991); by permission of the author.

Susan Frame: "Jutting Rock painting," HO (May 98); by permission of the artist.

D. Claire Gallagher: "Faint Rustle of Envelopes Rengay," F 19, no. 1 (1996); by permission of the author.

Larry Gates: "a cloud on the water," F 11, no. 3 (1988); by permission of the author.

Garry Gay: "Hole in the ozone," *Family Reunion* (n.p., 1999); "Weight lifter," FN; "Friday the 31st Rengay," F 22, no. 1 (1999); by permission of the author.

Joyce Austin Gilbert: "marshmallows melt," A 2 (1999); by permission of the author.

Lee Gurga: "trying the pump," MH 19, no. 1 (1988); "midnight," MH 31, no. 1 (2000); by permission of the author.

Yvonne Hardenbrook: "I can't stay," MH 30, no. 2 (1999) "French waiter," MH 30, no. 1 (1999); by permission of the author.

Lorraine Ellis Harr: "the time it takes," 70 Sevens Pathways of the Dragonfly (Middlewood, 1986); by permission of the author.

Peggy Heinrich: "Christmas eve," u.p.; by permission of the author.

Doris Heitmeyer: "On the morning bus," WFF; by permission of the author.

Christopher Herold: "while I'm gone," FN; by permission of the author.

Anna Holley: "If the moon," L 14, no. 1. (1999); "a long shadow," AT 6 (1999); by permission of the author.

A. Aiko Horiuchi: "lumpy birds sumi-e," tws; by permission of the artist.

Virgil Hutton: "Dusk over the lake," Midwest Haiku Anthology, ed. Randy Brooks and Lee Gurga (High/Coo, 1992); by permission of Lenore E. Hutton.

Hiromi Inoue: "jutting rock trans." and "blood-red skies trans.," HO (May 98); by permission of the translator.

Jim Kacian: "The Order of Stars," Six Directions: Haiku of the Local Ecology (Las Alameda, 1997); "Coast-to-Coast Renga," u.p.; by permission of the author.

Dennis Kalkbrenner: "Night Visitor," MH 29, no. 1 (1998); by permission of the author.

Leroy Kanterman, "Sunset," F 13, no. 3 (1990); by permission of the author.

Adele Kenny: "migrating geese," A Haiku Path, The Haiku Society of America 1968-1988 (Haiku Society of America, 1994); by permission of the author.

Michael Ketchek: "Chaco Canyon Haibun," MH 30, no. 1 (1998); by permission of the author.

Larry Kimmel: "crabapple petals everywhere," MH 31, no. 1 (2000); "when I think," TS; "all that I did today I did," F 22, no. 2 (1999); by permission of the author.

Karen Klein: "trees still bare sumi-e," AHH; "carved wooden bowl," P 3, no. 1 (1999); by permission of the artist.

Nancy Kline: "Coast-to-Coast Renga," u.p.; by permission of the author.

Kris Kondo: "renrepeat," OR; by permission of the author.

Rich Krivcher: "Friday the 31st Rengay," F 22, no. 1 (1999); by permission of the author.

Rick Kuntz: "Coast-to-Coast Renga," u.p.; by permission of the author.

Elizabeth Searle Lamb: "the old irrigation ditch," *Across the Windharp: Collected and New Haiku* (La Alameda, 1999); by permission of the author.

Watha Lambert: "it was spring," AT 7 (1999); by permission of the author.

Kenneth C. Leibman: "in front of," F 21, no. 1 (1998); by permission of the author.

Leatrice Lifshitz: "my tracks . . . their tracks," F 12, no. 2 (1989); by permission of the author.

Geraldine C. Little: "the bright silence," F 5, no. 3 (1982).

D. S. Lliteras: "Idiot," *Half Hidden by Twilight* (Hampton Roads, 1994); by permission of the author.

Tom Lynch: "xix-xxi," *Rain Drips from the Trees* (n.p., 1992); by permission of the author.

paul m.: "dawn," F 22, no. 1 (1999); by permission of the author.

Molly Magner: "the neglected garden," MH 29, no. 1 (1989); by permission of the author.

John Martone: "no one," MH 30, no. 2 (1999); by permission of the author.

Molly McGee: "the secret world," F 22, no. 2 (1999); by permission of the author.

Donald McLeod: "freeway begins," MH 29, no. 1 (1998); by permission of the author.

Michael McNierney: "wolf spider dancing," F 10, no. 4 (1987); by permission of the author.

Connie Meester: "box after box," AT 6 (1999); "breaking through rengay," F 22, no. 2 (1999); by permission of the author.

Carol Montgomery: "middle of the highway," I 4, no. 4 (1991); "fake cell phone," MH 30, no. 2 (1999); "between pinches of goldfish food," I 5, no. 2 (1992); by permission of the author.

Marlene Mountain: "cloudy day," F 13, no. 3 (1990); "frog," *The Haiku Anthology*, ed. Cor van den Heuvel (Simon & Schuster, 1986); "renrepeat," OR; "smoke from a neighbor's chimney," F 2, nos. 3–4 (1979); by permission of the author.

Jason Murray: "morning tea," A 2 (1999); by permission of the author.

Pamela Miller Ness: "We feed the ducks," AT 7 (1999); "early morning needle-point haiga," u.p.; by permission of the artist.

Charles D. Nethaway, Jr.: "waterfall at night," F 5, no. 4 (1982).

Patricia Neubauer: "Autumn afternoon," *Four Seasons*, ed. Kôko Katô (Seihodo, 1991); by permission of the author.

Donnie Nichols: "at the sushi bar," MH 30, no. 2 (1999); by permission of the author.

H. F. Noyes: "*Wabi* Suchness in Haiku," F 20, no. 3 (1997); by permission of the author.

Brent Partridge: "a passing shower," MH 31, no. 1 (2000); by permission of the author.

Yali Peng: "jutting rock calligraphy," HO (May 98); by permission of the calligrapher.

Alan Pizzarelli: "nightfall," MH 20, no. 2 (1989); by permission of the author.

Francine Porad: "twilight deepens," T 6 (1989); "yard sale," *Laddles and Jellyspoons* (Vandina, 1996); "cold November day," L 14, no. 1 (1999); "jutting rock," HO (May 98); "renrepeat," OR; "reverberations tan-renga," L (May 96); by permission of the author.

Robert Henry Poulin: "in the crystal vase," TS.

Gloria Procsal: "carrying home," F 22, no. 3 (1999); by permission of the author.

Tony Pupello: "so round moon," A 3 (1999); by permission of the author.

Carol Purington: "small clouds," F 22, no. 2 (1999); "remaining snow renku," F 22, no. 1 (1999); by permission of the author.

David Rice: "morning walk," AT 6 (1999); "Snow," *In Each Other's Footsteps* (Pressed for Time, 1996); by permission of the author.

Frank K. Robinson: "first flakes," F 7, no. 4 (1984); by permission of the author.

Emily Romano: "Strands," F 22, no. 2 (1999); by permission of the author.

Raymond Roseliep, "seance," *Rabbit in the Moon* (Alembic, 1983); by permission of Daniel J. Rogers.

Bruce Ross: "Head against head," HI 36 (1999); "country farm market," *The Scare Crow, A Collection of Haiku and Senryu*, ed. Leroy Kanterman (Red Moon,

1999); "bright spring day," MH 30, no. 3 (1999); "NO CRAB HUNTING," MH 27, no. 3 (1996); "the lumpy birds squat," tws; "autumn drizzle," NC 8, no. 1 (1991); "A Dirge for the Great Mother" and "luminous moonlight," TT; "mountain dusk," MH 30, no. 1 (1999); "Blackbirds," F 17, no. 2 (1994); "Boston T,'" *Raw Nervz Haiku* 6, no. 2 (2000); "Aglow," MH 25, no. 2 (1994); "spring chill," MH 23, no. 3 (1992); "abandoned house," *Haiku Moment, An Anthology of Contemporary North American Haiku*, ed. Bruce Ross (Charles E. Tuttle, 1993); "until we stop," F 22, no. 3 (1999); "The Haiku 'Moment' and Accuracy," MH 26, no.1 (1995); "bent over haiga," AHH2; "blue sky," "South Miami night," "Kindred Spirits," "this waiting," and "Coast-to-Coast Renga," u.p.; by permission of the author.

Murray David Ross: "Head against head *sumi-e*," u.p.; by permission of the artist.

Charles Rossiter: "so many favorites," MH 30, no. 2 (1999); by permission of the author.

Alexis Rotella: "California friends," MH 30, no. 2 (1999); "I don't mean" and "She's running for office," *Looking for a Prince* (White Peony, 1991); by permission of the author.

Hal Roth: "only a shanty," BS 2, no. 3 (1982); "Winter Haibun," MH 23, no. 2 (1992); by permission of the author.

Miriam Sagan: "The whole neighborhood," I 3, no. 4 (1987); by permission of the author.

Joan C. Sauer: "There, by the roadside," F 22, no. 3 (1999); by permission of the author.

Sally Secor: "A Garden Bouquet," *Wedge of Light*, ed. Michael Dylan Welch, Cor van den Heuvel, and Tom Lynch (Press Here, 1998); by permission of the author.

John Sheirer: "deep in the argument," F 21, no.3 (1998); by permission of the author.

Robert Spiess: "Becoming dusk," *The Shape of Water* (Modern Haiku, 1982); by permission of the author.

Joan Stamm: "Coast-to-Coast Renga," u.p.; by permission of the author.

R.A. Stefanac: "Ginkgo biloba," u.p.; by permission of the author.

John Stevenson: "nothing," P 1, no. 2 (1998); "tourist town," *Some of Silence* (Red Moon 1999); "Another Painting Renku," F 20, no. 1 (1997); "winter sun," F 23, no. 1 (2000); by permission of the author.

Ebba Story: "peeping . . . peeping," W 20 (1994); "Faint Rustle of Envelopes Rengay," F 19, no. 1 (1996); by permission of the author.

Christopher Suarez: "signing," F 17, no. 1 (1994); by permission of the author.

Kenneth Tanemura: "drone of a cricket song" and "alone in a crowd," *No Love Poems* (Small Poetry, 1994); by permission of the author.

Mary C. Taylor: "twilight *sumi-e*," P 3, no. 1 (1999); by permission of the artist.

John Thompson: "Friday the 31st Rengay," F 22, no. 1 (1999); by permission of the author.

Tom Tico: "Christmas Eve," MH 28, no. 1 (1997); by permission of the author.

vincent tripi: "waving back," BS 9, no. 2 (1994); by permission of the author.

Charles Trumbull: "angry at them too," A 3 (1999); by permission of the author.

Cor van den Heuvel: "a stick goes over," *Dark* (Chant, 1982); "melting snow," MH 22, no. 1 (1991); "tundra," *the window washer's pail* (Chant, 1963); by permission of the author.

Lequita Vance: "it was," WFF; by permission of the author.

Zeke Vayman: "Coast-to-Coast Renga," u.p.

Nick Virgilio: "Autumn twilight," *Selected Haiku* (Burnt Lake, 1985); by permission of Anthony Virgilio.

Eugenie Waldteufel: "november moon *sumi-e*," SXSE 4, no. 3 (1997); by permission of the artist.

Linda Jeannette Ward: "Laundry Day," F 22, no. 2 (1999); by permission of the author.

Michael Dylan Welch: "a new face on TV," MH 31, no. 1 (2000); "at his favorite deli," W 8 (1990); "church bells," F 22, no. 1 (1999); by permission of the author.

Paul O. Williams: "morning sun," F 22, no. 1 (1999); by permission of the author.

Thom Williams: "old white dogwood," P (Fall 1999); "by their winter lights," F 22, no. 23 (1999); by permission of the author.

John Wills: "touch of dawn," "dusk from rock," and "the hills," *Reed Shadows* (Burny Lake, 1987); by permission of Marlene Mountain.

Anita Wintz: "We walk this morning," F 20, no. 2 (1997); by permission of the author.

Also by Bruce Ross

HAIKU MOMENT

*An Anthology of Contemporary
North American Haiku*
By Bruce Ross

ISBN 0-8048-1820-7

The most comprehensive volume of
contemporary North American haiku
written in English, this book features
over 800 haiku by 185 poets.

JOURNEY TO THE INTERIOR

American Versions of Haibun
By Bruce Ross

ISBN 0-8048-3159-9

Haibun is a beautiful Japanese form of
autobiographical poetic prose accompanied by verse, usually haiku. This is
the first anthology specifically devoted
to original haibun written in English
and reflects some of the most moving,
personal, and spiritual literature being
produced today.

Also available from Tuttle Publishing

JAPANESE HAIKU
By Kenneth Yasuda

ISBN 0-8048-1096-6

The most authoritative and concise book
on Japanese haiku available: what it is, how
it developed, and how it is practiced in
both Japanese and English. One of the few
books to combine both translated haiku
with haiku written originally in English, this
is the perfect book for lovers of poetry who
do not have a solid background in haiku.

A BUTTERFLY

A falling flower, thought I,
Fluttering back to the
branch—
Was a butterfly.

—Moritake from *Japanese Haiku*

Also available from Tuttle Publishing

THE HAIKU BOX
By Lonnie Hull DuPont

ISBN 1-58290-030-2

This kit is the first of its kind—an attractive package that captures the creative and spiritual power of haiku. It is simple and fun to use, with fifty evocative word tiles and a blank journal. The enclosed book, *Footprints in the Snow*, provides a fascinating background on haiku, including many masterful examples and over two dozen exercises to awaken the poet within.

Also available from Tuttle Publishing

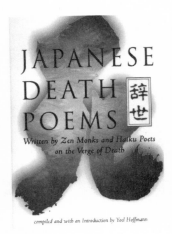

JAPANESE DEATH POEMS

Written by Zen Monks and Haiku Poets on the Verge of Death
Compiled and with an Introduction by Yoel Hoffmann

ISBN 0-8048-3179-3

From passionate samurai writings and meditative Zen haiku to the satirical poems of later centuries, hundreds of *jisei* (death poems) have been translated into English here, many for the first time. The result is a moving, powerful collection whose philosophical and aesthetic profundity will give readers pause.

CLASSIC HAIKU

A Master's Selection
Selected and Translated by Yuzuru Miura

ISBN 0-8048-1682-4

In this wonderful collection, haiku poet Yuzuru Miura has selected and trans-lated poems by past masters such at Basho and Buson, as well as contem-porary poets. Fireflies, pheasants, a summer shower, and other beautiful subjects are included among the one hundred poems in this impressive anthology. A revered collection, this book evokes the peace and serenity of the Japanese way of life.